THE MANTLE

Dr. Jeb Ihimekpen

DIVINE TOUCH BIBLE CHURCH INTL INC USA CHURCHES

Copyright © 2023 by Dr. Jeb Ihimekpen

All rights reserved. No part of this publication, The Mantle, may be reproduced, distributed, or transmitted in any form or by any means, including photocopying, recording, or other electronic or mechanical methods, without the prior written permission of the author, Dr. Jeb Ihimekpen, except in the case of brief quotations embodied in critical reviews and certain other noncommercial uses permitted by copyright law.

For permission requests, please contact the author or the church at the following address.

Contact Address:

Dr. Jeb Ihimekpen
Divine Touch Bible Church International Inc
102 Howard Street, Irvington, NJ 07111
+1 (973) 202-0411
https://www.dtbcusa.org
dtbcusa@gmail.com

This church worship manual is a work of faith and has been developed for use within the Divine Touch Bible Church International community. The contents, including prayers, songs, and liturgical elements, have been carefully selected and compiled by Dr. Jeb Ihimekpen and the Divine Touch Bible Church International Worship Committee.

Printed in the United States of America

PRELUDE

The Mantle is a structural guideline outlining how Divine Touch Bible Church International Inc. will be directed and spiritually managed in the United States of America. It covers all cross-sections, ranging from spiritual, physical, welfare, leadership, discipline, departmental designations, church administration, members' affairs, financial management, marital engagement, and relationships.

Bishop Oyedepo states, "It is the structure that determines the strength, growth, stability, and efficiency of any organization. It is structure first – not strength or skill, but structure! Every form of people-management requires a functional structure to run. Any system without an efficient structure is bound to rupture. Without a viable structure, there can be no enviable future for any organization."

God believes in structure. He Himself instituted an efficient structure for the church in the wilderness through Jethro, Moses' father-in-law (Exodus 18:21-24/Acts 7:38). The Holy Spirit also inspired the structuring of the Early Church (Acts 6:1-7).

From my findings, I have observed that growth without established goals is like constructing a building without a foundation, according to Matthew 7:24-27. This operational manual seeks, among other things, to establish the ministry of the church in the following ways: establish this commission in America at large, starting from New Jersey, and then across the 50 states of this country, and finally secure the posterity of this commission in the years to come (2 Peter 1:10).

Standardize the organizational structure and circulate it among the operators. This manual, called The Mantle, shall contain our doctrines, values, ministerial ethics, mysteries, training, and special services in full. The final goal of this manual shall be to move the commission from growth to establishment (Psalm 90:17).

TABLE OF CONTENTS

Prelude 2

Introduction - The Mantle 11

Foundation And History Of Divine Touch Bible Church Intl Inc 13

Formation- Federal, State And Irs 16

Organizational Structure 17

Vision, Mission Values And Statement Of Our Belief 19

    Our Vision 19

    Our Mission 20

    Statement Of Faith 20

The Constitution Of Divine Touch Bible Church 23

    Article 2.1 - Preamble 23

    Article 2.2 - Name: 23

    Article 2.3 - Registered Office: 23

    Article 2.4 - Aims And Objectives: 23

Bye Laws Of Divine Touch Bible Church 27

    Article I - Meetings 27

    Article Ii - Directors 29

    Article Iii - Officers 32

    Article Iv - Corporate Seal, Execution Of Instruments 33

Church Services And Programs 34

The Structure Of A Typical Church Service 37

    The Word And Prayer Emphasis 37

    Praise & Worship/Choir Ministration 37

    Opening Prayer 37

    Worship Offerings 37

    Testimonies 37

- Announcements 38
- Call To Worship 38
- Call To Prayer 38
- End Of The Month All Praise/Thanksgiving Service 38
- Further Provisions On Church Service 39

Church Service Units 40
- Aims: 40
- Basis: 40

Operational Units 42
- Prayer/Challengers'/Intercessors' Squad 42
- Evangelism Unit 42
- Follow-Up And Visitation Group 43
- Believers' Foundation Class 43
- Ushering & Protocol 44
- Sanctuary Keepers 45
- Security 46
- Hospitality & Medical Team 47
- Technical Team 48
- Transport Unit 49
- Children's Church Teachers 49
- Choir And Instrumentalists 50
- Decoration And Logistics Unit 53
- Media And Publicity Unit: 54

Definition Of Terms In The Leadership/General Church Forum 55
Leadership Of Service Units 56
- A. Service Unit Executives 56
- B. Terms Of Reference For The Executives Of The Unit 56
- C. Criteria For Nomination 56

- D. Nomination Process 57
- E. Monitoring And Record-Keeping 57

Central Church Appointed Positions 59
- The Resident Pastor 59
- The Associate Pastor 60
- The Evangelist 61
- Deacon And Deaconesses 62
- The Zonal Coordinators 63
- General Secretary 64
- Assistant General Secretary 65
- Financial Secretary 65
- Assistant Financial Secretary 65

Regional Level 66
- Office Of Directors: 66

Foundation Of Our Faith 71
- School Of Ministry: 71

Lesson 1 73
- Topic: Basic Bible Hermeneutics 73

Lesson 2 75
- Topic: Salvation 75

Lesson 3: 77
- Topic: Justification 77

Lesson 4 79
- Topic: Sanctification 79

Lesson 5 81
- Topic: Prayers 81

Lesson 6 83
- Topic: Scriptural Giving 83

Lesson 7 86
    Topic: Baptism 86

Lesson 8 88
    Topic: Communion 88

Lesson 9: Statement Of Faith 92

The Ordinance Of Water Baptism 95
    What Is Baptism? 95
    Water Baptism - Is It Required For Salvation? 95
    Significance Of Water Baptism 96
    Dtbc Doctrine On Baptism 96
    Administration Of Baptism 97

Ordinance Of Marriage 99
    Outlined Below Are Biblical Stands On Marriage: 99
    Biblical Purpose Of Marriage Includes: 100
    Administration Of Marriage - Member's Welfare 100
    Marriage Committee 100
    Procedure For Marriage 101
    Standard Marriage Preparation 103
    Purpose Of Marriage Counseling: 104
    Counseling Format: 106
    Duration Of Counseling 107
    Recommendation/Report 107
    Marriage Seminar Topics: 108
    Marriage Solemnization 108
    Wedding In Other Churches: 113
    Marriage To Unbelievers: 114
    Divorce In Christian Marriage: 114
    Same Sex Marriage 115

- Homegoing Program 116
  - Introduction 116
  - Burial Programs 117
- Membership Welfare Operations 120
  - Position Against Vows At All Levels 120
  - Sectional Ministries In The Church 120
  - Welfare Of Members 122
- Financial Management 124
- Monitoring And Record-Keeping 125
- Disapproved Practices 126
- Buildings And Car Dedication 127
- Child Covenant Naming And Dedication 128
  - Note Should Be Taken Of The Following: 128
  - Procedure 128
  - Child Covenant Naming Ceremony: 129
  - Covenant Naming Message 130
  - Child Dedication 130
- Discipline 131
  - Ministers - 8 Weeks: 131
  - Leaders - 6 Weeks: 131
  - Workers - 4 Weeks: 131
  - Members - 2 Weeks: 132
- Leadership Succession 133
- Divine Touch Bible Extensions In The Usa 134
- Divine Touch Bible Church Intl Inc Usa - Vision Ahead 135
  - 5-Year Plan 135
  - 10-Year Plan 135
  - 25-Year Plan 136

INTRODUCTION

The Mantle is a scriptural guide and operational tool that provides direction on how Divine Touch Bible Church International Inc., USA, will run, operate, and manage its churches. This tool will work in tandem with the constitution and operational instructions received from the headquarters church in Lagos, Nigeria.

The Mantle is written with the Kingdom at heart, Jesus as Lord, and winning souls for Christ as the ultimate purpose of the Church of Jesus Christ on earth. This Mantle will be reviewed annually by the Headquarters church and the regional headquarters based in the United States, as the Lord leads and inspires.

To all leaders, ministers, workers, members, associate members, and everyone called to this global commission, you are encouraged to follow this Mantle, along with the Holy Bible, in determining all operations in the church, both at the regional and branch levels.

Divine Touch Bible Church International Inc. is a church of Christ; thus, all intentions, attention, and dividends should profit Christ and Christ alone. With the help of the Holy Spirit, the Bible, and this operational manual, we will be able to present souls that are chaste and ready for the coming of our Master and Savior, Jesus Christ.

Apostle Paul spoke to Timothy in 1 Timothy 3:15,

> *"But if I tarry long, that thou mayest know how thou oughtest to behave thyself in the house of God, which is the church of the living God, the pillar and ground of the truth."*

This Mantle serves as a guide to moderate and oversee all operations in the Church of God, which is the ground and pillar of Truth. To this end, this Mantle is written so that Jesus Christ and His crucifixion may be glorified.

Amen.

Apostle Dr. Joseph Ihimekpen
Senior Pastor
Divine Touch Bible Church International Inc.
USA.

FOUNDATION AND HISTORY OF DIVINE TOUCH BIBLE CHURCH INTL INC.

Divine Touch Bible Church Intl Inc was founded by the Lord Jesus Christ through our Father in the Lord, Rev. Dr. and Rev. Mrs. Peter Odion Olumese, on September 5th, 2000. The vision of the church is to liberate souls that are in bondage by the liberating power of the Lord. Ever since its inception, the Lord has glorified Himself through the raw manifestation of His power.

Pastor Dr. Joseph Ihimekpen, who was a youth pastor in the Lagos church, relocated to the United States on August 20th, 2007. He believed that only sons of men would eventually become fathers of men. This led him to serve in a church in New Jersey called Christian Charismatic Pilgrims Mission (CCPM) for nine years under the leadership of Pastor Peace-Val Ekwe. After serving, he received a mandate to start Divine Touch Bible Church in the United States. He took appropriate permission with a one-year notice from the leading Pastor of CCPM, and on August 30th, 2016, he was granted a release and a prayerful send-off to go and do the bidding of the Heavenly Father.

House fellowship began with two families in attendance, with a few friends and neighbors making a total of 17 people, including children, present at the first meeting. Fellowship continued with aggressive evangelism, prayer meetings, and diligent teaching of the word. The home church grew to about 40 persons before being inaugurated on the 26th of March 2017 by the G.O. Rev Dr. Peter Olumese, who was represented by Bishop Chris.

Services continued on Wednesdays, tagged as "Hour of Divine Touch," and Sunday Encounter services. By the end of the first year, the church had grown to about 100 members in weekly attendance. By the end of the second year, membership continued to grow in leaps and bounds to about 200 members. Multiple services were then introduced to accommodate the growing membership. By the end of the fifth year, when this mantle was written, membership had grown to an average of 450 members and counting. No doubt, God has been our strength and the maker of every good and perfect blessing.

The leading Pastor of the New Jersey church, popularly called "Jesus' Errand Boy," has always reiterated the inspiration the Lord implanted in his heart when Divine Touch Bible Church USA was planted in New Jersey. He stated that this church would be like a seed planted and hidden, soon to become the mighty tree that would grow, expand, and provide shelter for the birds of the field. In other words, this church, which started small, would grow to become a mega church with a multitude of men, women, youth, and children. It would give birth to many churches and pastor many pastors.

Over the years, we have seen multiple manifestations of this vision, and many more are on the way. The history is nothing compared to the glory that lies ahead. Scriptures maintain, "For I reckon that the sufferings of this present time are not worthy to be compared with the glory which shall be revealed in us" (Rom 8:18). Jesus started this church, the Holy Spirit has been in charge, and we, His servants, are always at His command.

With the history in place, this mantle is here to provide directions to all future pastors, leaders, members, workers, and lovers of this commission that the Lord will add to this global commission in the years to come. Divine Touch Bible Church was registered in New Jersey on June 16th, 2016, and inaugurated on March 26th, 2017. The international church started in New Jersey, and by the grace of God, is expected to spread abroad according to the word of the Lord. The church, at five years old in New Jersey, is currently located in Newark, New Jersey, with a Pastor, several leaders, multiple workers, and a multitude of men and women attending both our on-ground and online weekly services. We gladly submit and maintain that Jesus Christ is the owner of this church, the Holy Spirit is the chief controller, and we are just His privileged servants.

FORMATION- FEDERAL, STATE AND IRS

Divine Touch Bible Church was officially registered at both federal and state levels on June 20th, 2016. The church obtained its approved 501(c)(3) status on August 20th, 2021. The home church began on September 5th, 2016, and was officially inaugurated on March 27th, 2017. As of the writing of this mantle, the church is five years old and is based in New Jersey, USA.

The church is owned by God, built by Jesus Christ, championed by the Holy Spirit, and has its headquarters in Lagos, Nigeria. There are no other affiliations other than those listed above.

ORGANIZATIONAL STRUCTURE

And I also say unto thee, that thou art Peter, and upon this rock, I will build my church; and the gates of hell shall not prevail against it." - Matthew 16:18.

Divine Touch Bible Church Int'l Inc., USA churches shall be operated via this organizational structure. The Holy Spirit is the ultimate personality that decides what we do on a daily, monthly, quarterly, and annual basis. The next personality shall be the General Overseer, Rev. Dr. and Rev. Mrs. Peter Olumese, both based in Lagos, Nigeria.

This shall be followed by the Senior Pastor of the USA churches, the Resident Pastors, the Associate Pastors, the Evangelist, the Teacher, the members of the leadership body. This shall be followed by the Board of Deacons and Deaconesses, then the workers, members in general, and finally, our associate and E-members.

The ideas, plans, programs, and activities can be initiated at any level, but final setting and approvals shall be completed from the Headquarters Church. As a branch church, our activities are regulated by the Headquarters Church via the General Overseer. As the USA church begins to grow into branches, there shall be regional engagement that will require the need for regional pastors and leaders. These shall be addressed in a later chapter.

Current Pastors, Associate Pastors, leaders, Deacons, and Deaconesses, workers, and members shall be under the spiritual watch of their direct Pastor but will be generally overseen by the General Overseer of Divine Touch Bible Church Int'l Inc., Nigeria.

Annual programs, anniversary events, and themes, as well as the watchword for the year, shall be obtained from the Headquarters Church. The weekly and monthly ministerial engagement shall be the sole responsibility of the Senior Pastor of the USA churches, with the help of the Holy Spirit under the guidelines of the Headquarters Church.

As we herald and maintain this confession in all of our services, "Jesus is the builder, and the Holy Spirit is the controller of the church," the Lord will indeed build His church, and the gate of hell shall not prevail against it.

VISION, MISSION, VALUES AND STATEMENT OF OUR BELIEF

Proverbs 29:18 - Where there is no vision, the people perish: but he that keeps the law, happy is he.

Habakkuk 2:3 - For the vision is yet for an appointed time, but at the end, it shall speak and not lie: though it tarry, wait for it; because it will surely come, it will not tarry.

Isaiah 29:11 - And the vision of all has become unto you as the words of a book that is sealed, which men deliver to one that is learned, saying, Read this, I pray thee: and he says, I cannot; for it is sealed.

Our Vision

The vision of a spiritual organization is the spiritual compass and guide that shows where the church is heading. Divine Touch Bible Church Intl Inc. USA has been empowered with the vision "To see all men saved and blessed to serve."

The logo of the church explains the vision in a pictorial format. The Bible is the living word of God that saves men, for there is no salvation in any other than Christ Jesus. He is the Word personified - John 1:1-3. When men are saved by faith in the Lord Jesus, who is the Word Himself, they are then blessed by the good hand of the Lord. Scriptures maintain, "You open your hand, and the desires of men are satisfied" - Psalms 145:16. We are saved by the Word, blessed by the hand of the Lord, and enflamed by the Holy Ghost to serve God and humanity.

Our Mission

The vision above shall be accomplished as we embrace the three mission values below:

A.	We strive and envision being the gateway to heaven by preaching the undiluted word of God.

B.	We strive and envision being the gateway to success by the application of a practical approach to success via the Word with demonstration.

C.	We strive and envision being the gateway to an impactful life by ministering to the spiritual and physical needs of humanity.

The above is what shapes our programs, teachings, messages, and general operations of the church. Everyone that the Lord brings and has resolved to grow with the church has to be taught our doctrinal beliefs, vision, and mission values. Details of becoming a member will be addressed much later. The statements listed below are our statement of faith as a church and a member of the body of Christ.

Statement of faith

We believe in, and live by, God the Father Almighty, maker of Heaven and earth, and in Jesus Christ, His Son, and our Lord who was conceived by the Holy Ghost through the Word of God and born of the Virgin Mary. He suffered under Pontius Pilate, was crucified, dead, and buried. He descended into Hell and He stripped Satan of his power. Upon the Third day, He rose again and ascended into Heaven where He is seated at the right hand of God the Father Almighty. We believe in the Holy Ghost, the worldwide body of Christ (His Church), the forgiveness of all sins, the resurrection of the dead, the communion of the saints, and life everlasting. We believe that through a profession of faith (trust) in the shed blood of Jesus Christ, His death, burial, resurrection, and ascension; one may become a partaker of their inheritance in Him.

1. We believe that the Bible is the inspired Word of God written by holy men as they were instructed by God. It is the inherent Word of God (II Tim 3:16).

2. We believe that man was created good and upright, for God said, "Let us make man in our own image, after our likeness". But man, voluntarily transgressed against God, and God has provided man with his only hope of salvation and redemption which is in Jesus Christ, the Son of God (Gen 1:26-31; 3:17; Rom 5:12-21).

3. We believe that Jesus came as a man, was born of a virgin, and His father is God. We believe that Jesus was born without the inherited sin of Adam and, during his entire life, committed no sin. Jesus was the eternal Father made visible, apart from whom there is no God (I Tim 3:16; John 10:30; Isaiah 9:6; Luke 2:11; Rev 1:8). We believe in the personal salvation of believers through the confession of sins, recognizing that Jesus Christ is the substitute for our sins, through his shed blood. It is by the grace of God, through faith in Jesus Christ and His shed blood that we become an heir of God (Rom 10:9,10; I John 1:9; Eph 2: 8-9).

4. We believe that the new birth is a direct witness of the Spirit and is an inward confession of Jesus Christ (Rom 8:16). We believe that following salvation through Jesus Christ, you should be baptized, as commanded by the Lord Jesus. This was the command He left His apostles. "Go ye therefore, and teach all nations, baptizing them, in the name of the Father, and the Son and the Holy Ghost" (Matt 28:19). Mark 16:16 reads, "He that believeth, and is baptized, shall be saved…"

5. We believe in divine healing through faith and that healing is a benefit of the atonement.

6. We believe in the nine gifts of the Holy Spirit and that these gifts are given throughout the Body of Christ and are in operation today (I Cor 12).

7. We believe in the imminent return, second coming of our Lord Jesus Christ for His Church (His Bride).

8. We believe that there is heaven and hell. Heaven is a place of eternal rest for the righteous (those who have accepted Jesus Christ as atonement for their sins) and hell is a place of eternal damnation for the unrighteous (those who do not accept Jesus Christ as their Lord and Savior) (Matt 28:19; Mark 16:16).

9. We believe in the millennial reign of Jesus, the revelation of the Lord Jesus Christ from heaven, and the millennial reign of Christ and his followers on earth (II Thes 1:7; Rom 11:26-27; Rev 20:1-7).

10. We believe in the Great Commission, to minister God's saving Grace and to reach out to the poor and lost in spirit (Mark 16:15). And foremost, to honor and obey God's command, "take the Gospel into all the world."

THE CONSTITUTION OF DIVINE TOUCH BIBLE CHURCH

Article 2.1 - Preamble

This body, set forth as DIVINE TOUCH BIBLE CHURCH INTL INC, hereby establishes and adopts the following Constitution called 'The Mantle.'

Article 2.2 - Name:

2.2.1 This Mission shall be known and called DIVINE TOUCH BIBLE CHURCH INTL INC.

Article 2.3 - Registered Office:

The Registered Office of the Church shall be situated in Nigeria and other regional locations where the Church operates.

Article 2.4 - Aims and Objectives:

The aims and objectives for which the Church is established are to:

2.4.1 Embark on evangelical missions and programs throughout the world to win souls for the Lord Jesus Christ and prepare men and women for the second coming of our Lord Jesus Christ.

2.4.2 Organize prayer meetings, establish prayer camps, and conduct prayer sessions on any matter at any place and for any adequate period.

2.4.3 Organize Bible Studies, teachings, seminars, discussions, and other programs to facilitate the study of the Bible.

2.4.4 Embark upon the planting, establishment, or building of Churches, Chapels, or any other place for Christian worship in any part of the world, to be known and called Divine Touch Bible Church, and to administer the same in accordance with Biblical principles.

2.4.5 Confer or permit to be conferred on the ministers (male or female) or staff (male or female) of the Church such titles, honor, names, awards, rights, or privileges if and when earned or due in accordance with biblical and ecclesiastical order or in line with the provisions of this Constitution for both men and women.

2.4.6 Publish or cause to be published in any place and at any time Christian literature, including tracts, magazines, periodicals, circulars, books, stickers, or make other publications, publicity, and expressions as may be conducive with its aims and objectives herein.

2.4.7 Make broadcasts, announcements, advertisements, or otherwise make publications of its programs through any medium, including social media and other digital platforms, in connection with Christian teachings, witnessing, doctrines, and Bible knowledge for the purpose of evangelization and promotion of the Christian Faith and making known the Lord Jesus Christ throughout the world.

2.4.8 Hold crusades, camp meetings, gatherings, conventions, fellowships, conferences, and other meetings by whatever name they are called for the pursuance of its objectives.

2.4.9 Organize Christian counseling, follow-up, teachings, trainings, seminars, symposia, and other similar programs for the benefit of its members and other persons.

2.4.10 Encourage the study, understanding, and practical application of Bible truth in everyday life.

2.4.11 Promote mutual understanding, love, peace, and unity among men.

2.4.12 Promote and propagate, or cause the same to be done, the growth of Christians and Christianity.

2.4.13 Cooperate with anybody or bodies whose aims and objectives are identical with or complementary to the Church's.

2.4.14 Acquire, own, possess or otherwise hold interest in any properties, including land, and have rights, title, license, and interests in any properties whatsoever.

2.4.15 Engage and participate in and encourage charitable, benevolent, and other merciful activities towards all men and especially those of the household of faith, in any part of the world.

2.4.16 Undertake, promote, develop and carry out charitable, educational, Christian religious, and scientific programs in line with our objectives to enhance the quality of life and well-being of individuals and communities in Nigeria, the United States, and the world at large.

2.4.17 Adopt all such means as the Church may think fit to generate funds for its objectives and to accept donations, subscriptions, gifts, collections, offerings, tithes, aids, allowances, and to sell and dispose of all real or personal property of the Church or any part thereof for the purpose of the objectives.

2.4.18 Purchase or take on lease or under lease or otherwise acquire any land, warehouses, mills, houses, or other buildings or any other real or personal property of any kind whatsoever and to erect, equip, maintain, manage, alter, pull down, enlarge, develop, and improve the same, and to acquire rights and privileges in relation to any land or buildings for the purpose of its objectives.

2.4.19 Secure any legislative or governmental authority or any license or franchise that is conducive to the interest of the Church and to enter any contract with persons, partners, companies, or government authorities which is beneficial to the Ministry.

BYE LAWS OF DIVINE TOUCH BIBLE CHURCH

The name of the organization is DIVINE TOUCH BIBLE CHURCH INTL INC. The organization is organized in accordance with the New Jersey Statutes, Title 15 A, as amended. The organization has not been formed for the making of any profit or personal financial gain. The assets and income of the organization shall not be distributed to or benefit the trustees, directors, or officers or other individuals. The assets and income shall only be used to promote corporate purposes as described below. Nothing contained herein, however, shall be deemed to prohibit the payment of reasonable compensation to employees and independent contractors for services provided for the benefit of the organization. This organization shall not carry on any other activities not permitted to be carried on by an organization exempt from federal income tax. The organization shall not endorse, contribute to, work for, or otherwise support (or oppose) a candidate for public office.

The purpose of the organization is the following: Worship of the Living God through praises, prayers, and preaching of the word of God. The organization is organized exclusively for purposes pursuant to section 501(c)(3) of the Internal Revenue Code.

Article I - Meetings

Section 1. Annual Meeting

An annual meeting shall be held once each calendar year for the purpose of electing directors and for the transaction of such other business as may properly come before the meeting. The annual meeting shall be held at the time and place designated by the Board of Directors from time to time.

Section 2. Special Meetings

Special meetings may be requested by the President or the Board of Directors. A special meeting of members is not required to be held at a geographic location if the meeting is held by means of the internet or other electronic communications technology in a manner pursuant to which the members can read or hear the proceedings substantially concurrent with the occurrence of the proceedings, vote on matters submitted to the members, pose questions, and make comments.

Section 3. Notice

Written notice of all meetings shall be provided under this section or as otherwise required by law. The Notice shall state the place, date, and hour of the meeting, and if for a special meeting, the purpose of the meeting. Such notice shall be mailed to all directors of record at the address shown on the corporate books, at least 10 days prior to the meeting. Such notice shall be deemed effective when deposited in ordinary U.S. mail, properly addressed, with postage prepaid.

Section 4. Place of Meeting

Meetings shall be held at the organization's principal place of business unless otherwise stated in the notice. Unless the articles of incorporation or bylaws provide otherwise, the board of directors may permit any or all directors to participate in a regular or special meeting by, or conduct the meeting using, any means of communication by which all directors participating may simultaneously hear each other during the meeting. A director participating in a meeting by this means shall be deemed to be present in person at the meeting.

Section 5. Quorum

Most of the directors shall constitute a quorum at a meeting. In the absence of a quorum, most of the directors may adjourn the meeting to another time without further notice. If a quorum is represented at an adjourned meeting, any business may be transacted that might have been transacted at the meeting as originally scheduled. The directors present at a meeting represented by a quorum may continue to transact business until adjournment, even if the withdrawal of some directors results in representation of less than a quorum.

Section 6. Informal Action

Any action required to be taken, or which may be taken, at a meeting, may be taken without a meeting and without prior notice if a consent in writing, setting forth the action so taken, is signed by the directors with respect to the subject matter of the vote.

Article II - Directors

Section 1. Number of Directors

The organization shall be managed by a Board of Directors consisting of 6 directors.

Section 2. Election and Term of Office

The directors shall be elected at the annual meeting. Each director shall serve a term of 2 years, or until a successor has been elected and qualified.

Section 3. Quorum

A majority of directors shall constitute a quorum.

Section 4. Adverse Interest

In the determination of a quorum of the directors, or in voting, the disclosed adverse interest of a director shall not disqualify the director or invalidate his or her vote.

Section 5. Regular Meeting

The Board of Directors shall meet immediately after the election for the purpose of electing its new officers, appointing new committee chairpersons, and for transacting such other business as may be deemed appropriate. The Board of Directors may provide, by resolution, for additional regular meetings without notice other than the notice provided by the resolution.

Section 6. Special Meeting

Special meetings may be requested by the President, Vice-President, Secretary, or any two directors by providing five days' written notice by ordinary United States mail, effective when mailed. Minutes of the meeting shall be sent to the Board of Directors within two weeks after the meeting. A special meeting of members is not required to be held at a geographic location if the meeting is held by means of the internet or other electronic communications technology in a manner pursuant to which the members can read or hear the proceedings substantially concurrent with the occurrence of the proceedings, vote on matters submitted to the members, pose questions, and make comments.

Section 7. Procedures

The vote of a majority of the directors present at a properly called meeting at which a quorum is present shall be the act of the Board of Directors, unless the vote of a greater number is required by law or by these by-laws for a particular resolution. A director of the organization who is present at a meeting of the Board of Directors at which action on any corporate matter is taken shall be presumed to have assented to the action taken unless their dissent shall be entered in the minutes of the meeting. The Board shall keep written minutes of its proceedings in its permanent records.

Section 8. Informal Action

Any action required to be taken at a meeting of directors, or any action which may be taken at a meeting of directors or of a committee of directors, may be taken without a meeting if a consent in writing setting forth the action so taken is signed by all of the directors or all of the members of the committee of directors, as the case may be.

Section 9. Removal / Vacancies

A director shall be subject to removal, with or without cause, at a meeting called for that purpose. Any vacancy that occurs on the Board of Directors, whether by death, resignation, removal or any other cause, may be filled by the remaining directors. A director elected to fill a vacancy shall serve the remaining term of his or her predecessor, or until a successor has been elected and qualified.

Section 10. Committees

To the extent permitted by law, the Board of Directors may appoint from its members a committee or committees, temporary or permanent, and designate the duties, powers, and authorities of such committees.

Article III - Officers

Section 1. Number of Officers

The officers of the organization shall be a President, one or more Vice Presidents (as determined by the Board of Directors), a Treasurer, and a Secretary. Two or more offices may be held by one person. The President may not serve concurrently as a Vice President.

President/Chairman: The President shall be the chief executive officer and shall preside at all meetings of the Board of Directors and its Executive Committee if such a committee is created by the Board.

Vice President: The Vice President shall perform the duties of the President in the absence of the President and shall assist that office in the discharge of its leadership duties.

Secretary: The Secretary shall give notice of all meetings of the Board of Directors and Executive Committee, shall keep an accurate list of the directors, and shall have the authority to certify any records, or copies of records, as the official records of the organization. The Secretary shall maintain the minutes of the Board of Directors' meetings and all committee meetings.

Treasurer/CFO: The Treasurer shall be responsible for conducting the financial affairs of the organization as directed and authorized by the Board of leaders and Executive Committee, if any, and shall make reports of corporate finances as required, but no less often than at each meeting of the Board of Directors and Executive Committee.

Section 2. Election and Term of Office

The officers shall be elected annually by the Board of leaders at the first meeting of the year, immediately following the annual meeting. Each officer shall serve a 2-year term or until a successor has been elected and qualified.

Section 3. Removal or Vacancy

The Board of Directors shall have the power to remove an officer or agent of the organization. Any vacancy that occurs for any reason may be filled by the Board of Directors.

Article IV - Corporate Seal, Execution of Instruments

1. The organization shall not have a corporate seal.
2. All instruments that are executed on behalf of the organization, which are acknowledged and affect an interest in real estate, shall be executed by the President or any Vice-President, and the Secretary or Treasurer.
3. All other instruments executed by the organization, including a release of mortgage or lien, may be executed by the President or any Vice President.
4. Notwithstanding the preceding provisions of this section, any written instrument may be executed by any officer(s) or agent(s) that are specifically designated by resolution of the Board of Directors.

CHURCH SERVICES AND PROGRAMS

Aims: To ensure maximum release of blessings upon the congregation in each service, it is essential to maintain orderliness, decency, and timeliness in all our church meetings. Every service shall be propelled towards bringing this mandate of Deliverance to fulfillment.

Types of Services: As a means of ministering to the congregation, we hold a series of services through which the blessings of the Lord are made available to the people.

Our services are broadly classified into two categories:

- a) Weekly Services
- b) Specialized Services

A. Weekly Services:

  i. Sunday Service – held on Sundays.
  ii. Midweek Prayer and Fasting/Bible studies.
  iii. Daily Morning Devotion from Monday to Saturday (Digital/online)
  iv. Counseling and Deliverance Meeting on Tuesday and Thursday

B. Specialized Services:

  i. Special Monthly Sunday Communion Service - Second Sunday of the month
  ii. Special Monthly Sunday Power Service - First Sunday of the Month
  iii. Special Thanksgiving and Children Dedication Service – Last Sunday of the month

C. Quarterly Meetings:

    1. 14 days Fasting and Prayers - January of every year
    2. 21 Days Fasting and Prayers - May of every year
    3. 30 days Fasting and Prayers - September of every year

D. Specialized Programs:

1. Marriage and Single Seminar - This is a special event where single individuals and married couples are taught the word of the Lord, coupled with counseling, prayers, and charge. This event takes place the first and second weekend in the month of June. Marriage Seminar on the first Saturday followed by Single on the next.
2. I Must Carry My Samuel - This is a special program for all our expectant mothers. It is an annual program where the mother of the Lord will be taught to stir up the faith of the participants, followed by a life-applicable teaching, counseling, and prayers. This event takes place on the first Saturday in the month of February.
3. Specialized Seminars - There shall be specialized seminars year-round to address concerns in the lives of members, with concerns not limited to immigration, real estate, taxation, career development, business acquisition, and self-empowerment, to mention but a few.
4. Men's Day Celebration - This group comprises all fathers in the church, both single and married fathers. They gather in an atmosphere of worship, prayers, thanksgiving, general presentation, and celebration. This event takes place annually on the third Sunday in the month of June.
5. Mother's Day Celebration - This is the gathering of all mothers in the church in an atmosphere of worship, prayers, thanksgiving, general presentation, and celebration. This event takes place annually on the second Sunday in the month of May.

6. Youth's Day Celebration - This category comprises youth ages 21-40 who are unmarried. This annual event takes place on the first Sunday in the month of August.
7. Teenagers Day Celebration - This is an annual event where the teenagers in the church, ages 9-20, will be celebrated. This usually takes place in the first week of July.
8. Children's Day Celebration - This is the event where all the children in the church, ages 0-8 years, will be celebrated. This event takes place in May of every year, precisely the last Sunday in the month of May.
9. Annual Picnic Event - This is an event where the church shall gather in an outdoor meeting. It shall be held once a year, precisely the first week in August.
10. Pastor's Appreciation - This is the event where the pastor is celebrated and appreciated. This usually takes place in August of every year.
11. Annual Convention/Anniversary - March of every year
12. This is when the anniversary of the church is to be celebrated. The last weekend in the month of March.

End of the Year Event:

1. 7 Sundays of Wonders event
2. Annual Thanksgiving/Banquet service
3. SHAMMAH - International Annual Program - Gathering of all Divine Touch Members for a period of retreat.

THE STRUCTURE OF A TYPICAL CHURCH SERVICE

The Word and Prayer Emphasis

The Mantle shows that the Word of Power, coupled with prayers, are the tools that bring about Deliverance. It directly implies that the point of emphasis in any service to bring about Deliverance should be the Word and Prayer (Rom. 10:17). The time allotted for the Word and its ministration or impartation in any service should occupy a prominent portion of the service.

Praise & Worship/Choir Ministration

This prepares the hearts of the people to receive the Word of Power and propels the hand of God to be evident in any service (Psalm 22:3).

Opening Prayer

Opening prayer shall be concise and proportional to service time.

Worship Offerings

Offering is not the focus of our services. Therefore, minimum time should be spent on blessing and receiving offerings.

Testimonies

The testimony of Jesus is the Spirit of prophecy. This means that every testimony shared can reproduce itself in other lives. It also helps to confirm the efficacy of God's word. It should be sharp and short. Therefore, service time allotted here should be moderated and not too long.

Announcements

Announcements should be typed and vetted by the Head of the station and would only require to be read. It should not be more than 5 minutes. Online platforms shall be provided to help pass across the volume of announcements, especially as it relates to service units, job vacancies, marriage intentions, special programs, and on-demand information, etc., that cannot be announced from the altar.

Call to Worship

The passage to be read should be relevant to the message and shall be derived from the book of Psalms, except where otherwise instructed.

Call To Prayer

One of the passages read from the call to worship shall be utilized to stir up the hearts of the people to pray. This should last for 5 minutes.

End of the Month All Praise/Thanksgiving Service

As a tradition, this Church has set aside the last Sunday of every month as a day to return to God with thanksgiving through an all praise-filled service for all his blessings during the month (Lk.17:11-19, Isa. 35:10). On such occasions, the message could be reduced by 10-15 mins. The schedule of service on Thanksgiving Day is as indicated in the general sample program.

Further Provisions on Church Service

The Church program content of all local assemblies is to be universal. For this reason, every station must submit to the Provincial Head Office the program plan of its special activities in the year following a declaration of the general themes. All local assemblies are expected to develop programs which follow after the monthly declaration at their various levels. Where central teaching guidelines are provided, strict adherence must be observed.

All stations shall be expected to obtain specific instructions from appropriate quarters as it relates to regular or special services for each year, such as seminars and special ministration services (e.g., anointing, Power services, holy communion, impartation services, etc.).

Pastors and leaders are required to observe the blessedness of keeping to time as scheduled for our services. This allows them to raise a responsible congregation, which can plan their lives as a requirement for excellent pursuit of purpose. Therefore, all Pastors are to observe that timeliness is an asset when applied with discipline.

CHURCH SERVICE UNITS

Jesus declared there is a work set before me, and I am ready to be stretched until it has been accomplished. It is required, therefore, that everyone who truly serves the Lord Christ should be engaged in a department of service. As a church, it is required that everyone who indicates interest in belonging to a department should go through the Believer's School of Ministry. Post-graduation, they are hereby released to serve in a department of their choice. The following departments are available as of the time of the production of this Mantle.

Aims:

- To harness properly the members of every congregation into active involvement in the service of the Vineyard.
- To ensure the effectiveness of the service units in every congregation.
- To ensure orderliness and neatness in their operations.

Basis:

Service is one of the fora through which God blesses His people and makes them more productive. It is, therefore, necessary to make and lay down some guidelines to achieve this (John 15:2,16).

- All service units will have the privilege of pastoral oversight for spiritual enhancement.
- All service units shall have a Leader.
- Selecting leaders of each unit must be done under the supervision of the Unit's Overseer or the Resident Pastor.
- Units led by any of the leadership members shall be self-existing, while units led by a non-leadership member

must be overseen by an ordained leader of the church or the Resident Pastor.

OPERATIONAL UNITS

Prayer/Challengers'/Intercessors' Squad

To stand in the gap in prayer for the church and members.

Operations of the Prayer Unit

1. This unit shall gather on a weekly basis, and also on demand as the Lord directs.
2. The focus of the unit shall be to pray for the church, which includes the pastors, leaders, workers, and members.
3. The unit shall also be able to engage in fasting, prayer camps, and vigils as the Lord directs.
4. The unit coordinator shall direct the affairs of this unit within the guidelines of this Mantle and the supervision of the Resident Pastor.

Evangelism Unit

To reach out to lost souls for the purpose of harvesting them into the church.

Operations of the Evangelism Unit

1. This unit shall be responsible for the weekly, monthly, and quarterly evangelistic outreach of the church.
2. The unit shall also be responsible for regularly taking the oversight of the church growth indices as described in the later part of this book.
3. This unit shall also take the lead in the church's general evangelistic outreaches.

4. The unit coordinator shall direct the affairs of this unit within the guidelines of this Mantle and the supervision of the Resident Pastor.

Follow-up and Visitation Group

responsible for following up the establishment of new converts and looking after their well-being.

Operations of the Follow-up & Visitation Unit

1. The unit shall be responsible for welcoming first-timers into the church, describing the church activities and programs.
2. This unit shall also be responsible for ensuring the first-timers' cards are properly filled, and all questions are answered.
3. This unit shall also ensure to follow up with the first-timers 24 hours post-service, 72 hours later, and 24 hours before the next service.
4. This unit shall take the lead in the zonal divisions of the general membership.
5. This unit shall also be responsible for assigning the first-timers to zones and report to the zonal coordinator.
6. The unit coordinator shall direct the affairs of this unit within the guidelines of this Mantle and the supervision of the Resident Pastor.

Believers' Foundation Class

This class aims to nurture new converts in the faith and enlighten first-time worshippers about the mandate of the Church.

Operations of the BFC Unit

1. This unit shall ensure that new believers and newcomers attend the believer's class.
2. The class will run for six weeks, covering content relevant to the mission assignment of this commission. More details can be found later in this book.
3. Participants in this program will graduate and be empowered to serve in different capacities at the church central.
4. The unit coordinator will teach the first five classes, while the resident pastor will conclude the class, detailing the vision, mission assignment, and statement of faith of this commission.
5. The unit coordinator will direct the affairs of this unit within the guidelines of this Mantle and under the supervision of the Resident Pastor.
6. The material covered will be the believers' foundation course outline, described later in this Mantle.

Ushering & Protocol

This team's role is to receive, direct, and guide worshippers to their seats and ensure general orderliness during service. The Protocol members welcome special guests and provide relevant information to worshippers.

Operations of the Ushering and Protocol Unit

1. The Ushering team will ensure that people are properly welcomed and directed to their appropriate seating positions.
2. Ushering members will strive to be in church on time, observe a moment of prayer, and plan their operations accordingly.

3. The ushers will also manage traffic between church services.
4. Ushers will ensure members are properly directed during times of giving, providing appropriate envelopes, and managing the offering box according to the financial team's direction.
5. Ushers will be active and sensitive during times of ministration, ensuring the safety of all those under the power and influence of the Holy Spirit.
6. The Protocol team will operate under the direction of the Ushering ministry. The Protocol team will ensure access to the altar area and the Pastor is well-controlled.
7. The Protocol team will also direct members to and from the Pastor during any services.
8. The Protocol team will ensure all required elements and materials for every service are provided. This includes, but is not limited to, proper microphones, water, and face towels.
9. The unit coordinator will direct the affairs of this unit within the guidelines of this Mantle and under the supervision of the Overseer or the Resident Pastor.

Sanctuary Keepers

This group is responsible for maintaining the general cleanliness of the auditorium and church premises.

Operations of the Sanctuary Keeper's Unit

1. This unit will be responsible for the general cleanliness and maintenance of the church, both inside and out.
2. The church auditorium and premises are to be kept clean after every service and before the next service.

3. This unit will also ensure all bathrooms are kept clean before and after services.
4. This unit will regularly meet to plan cleaning and maintenance activities.
5. The unit coordinator will direct the affairs of this unit within the guidelines of this Mantle and under the supervision of the Resident Pastor.

Security

The purpose of this unit is to ensure the safety of life and property within and around the premises during church services. This unit shall serve as both the Security & Traffic team.

Operations of the Security and Traffic Team

1. This unit shall work hand-in-hand with the ushering team.
2. The unit shall be responsible for the physical safety of life and property on the church premises, including the main sanctuary and the parking lot.
3. The team shall direct all cars where to park and exit the premises.
4. The team shall handle any disorderly persons in the church auditorium and premises; if there is any chance of escalation, law enforcement shall be contacted.
5. In the event of a collision between vehicles of the brethren, the direct traffic control should report such event to the head of the unit for possible resolution between both parties. If there is defiance from any of the affected parties, law enforcement shall be involved.
6. This unit shall be answerable to the Resident Pastor, Regional Coordinator, or Regional Pastor.

7. This unit shall have access to a two-to-multi-system communication device throughout the course of the service.
8. This unit shall also have access to the security systems to review the services and operations of the service. In the event of occurrences in any service, a briefing will be done, and a review will be completed to replan and regroup.

Hospitality & Medical Team

The purpose of this unit is to attend to the welfare of worshippers and to provide first aid attendance to medical emergencies during church services.

Operations of the Hospitality & Medical Unit

1. This unit shall be responsible for the general welfare of the church, from the pastor to the least member.
2. This unit shall ensure to follow up with all members who are absent from the church, confirming their welfare; if sick, visits should be coordinated accordingly.
3. This unit shall also ensure that new mothers and their newborns are properly visited. The first visit must be completed after the birth of the child at the hospital, and another visit must be coordinated when the mother and newborn return home.
4. This unit shall assess the new mother's coping skills; if unable to care for the baby independently, an appropriate report should be given to the First Lady for proper follow-up.
5. This unit shall operate with a high level of sensitivity. If the person to be visited is male, no single female should be allowed to complete the visit. If there are no

brothers to accompany a sister, two sisters can go and should not spend more than 10 minutes on such visits.
6. This unit shall be headed by a Leader or Coordinator and will work in proximity with the Pastor and the general membership. A yearly report will be submitted to the Pastor.

Technical Team

The purpose of this unit is to ensure the effective functioning of the carpentry, plumbing, and electrical equipment during church services. This unit shall function in tandem with the Media unit.

Operations of the Technical Team

1. This unit shall be responsible for the effective functioning of all plumbing systems in the church, ensuring timely maintenance schedules. This includes bathroom/toilet plumbing units and heating and cooling system devices.
2. This unit shall also be responsible for the effective functioning of all electrical devices, ensuring that they are all in working condition. The team shall ensure that sockets are all covered and that the safety of all electrical devices is maintained.
3. This unit shall be responsible for ensuring that all necessary electrical repairs are corrected in a timely manner.
4. This unit shall also ensure that all carpentry aspects of the church building, both within and without, are safe for operations. This includes walls, staircases, church frontage, altar, and children's areas. The team shall ensure that all necessary carpentry repairs are completed in a timely manner.

5. . This unit shall also be responsible for taking a timely and complete inventory of the ministry's physical properties.
6. This unit shall submit a yearly annual report to the Resident Pastor.

Transport Unit

To ensure easy commuting of worshippers to and from church.

Operations of the Transport Unit

1. This unit shall be solely responsible for pickup and drop off of all members that are not yet driving.
2. This unit shall coordinate their activities in a timely manner, ensuring that commuters and drivers are both in church on time for their services.
3. This unit shall also ensure that the church van is well maintained, ensuring that all necessary repairs are completed in a timely manner.

Children's Church Teachers

To ensure the smooth running of the children's unit of the church and to present the gospel to the children at their level of understanding. This unit shall be responsible for the spiritual coordination, conduct, and teaching of our children.

Operations of the Children's Teachers

1. The following children in this age range will be in the class - Ages 1 to 8 years.
2. The actual class covers ages 3 to 8; the coordinator shall ensure accurate record-keeping of the children's lists and know when children below this age bracket can be

added. They should also know when children older than the age bracket should be prayed for and released to the next spiritual group.
3. This unit shall ensure timely arrival at assigned services, prepare the class, and be ready to receive the children on time and release them back to the church after the class teaching.
4. This unit shall also ensure the preparation of children for events in the church, especially major programs and Children's Day celebrations.
5. This unit shall also ensure the preparation of children for their summer trip; teachers are also to chaperone the children on the trip.
6. In the event of any negative occurrence(s) in any of the classes, such incidents should be reported to the coordinator, and such should be reported to the Resident Pastor at the end of the service.
7. The children's teachers shall be answerable to the unit coordinator; the coordinator shall be answerable to the Resident Pastor, Regional Coordinator, or Regional Pastor.

Choir and Instrumentalists

To minister in songs and lead worshippers in praise and worship sessions.

1. The choir ministry shall be called - Echoes of Glory (Psalms 29:9)
2. The choir ministry shall manage two major ministries
    a. The ministrations of divinely inspired songs
    b. The instrumentalists
3. The unit shall be headed by a director with an assistant and secretary.

4. The choir director shall also oversee the head of the instrumentalists.
5. The choir director shall be under the overall supervision of the overseer of the unit.
6. The choir director shall be chosen by the people, screened by the Overseer, and approved by the Pastor.

These shall be the qualities of the choir director

- Be born again with visible fruit of righteousness - Galatians 5:22
- Be present at all services.
- Has been in the church for more than 2 years.
- Be down to earth, humble, teachable, and handle pressure with simplicity.
- Be a disciplinarian by lifestyle
- Can flow in this unique ministry.

This position is valid for 2 years and renewable once.

(a) The choir director has the capacity to address the instrumentalists, also has the capacity to install or replace the head of the instrumentalists after all due process has been put in place, which includes informing the overseer and obtaining approval from the resident pastor.

(b) The choir ministry shall operate in this manner:

1. Be available to rehearse and practice towards their ministration every Saturday at the agreed time.

2. Every member of the choir is expected to be on time at their agreed time of meeting, and if any delay, inform the appropriate personnel.

3. The choir meeting should not exceed 3 hours except for the preparation towards special events.

4. The choir director shall be allowed to introduce a godly rule that will ensure the choir ministry is up to the divine task ahead of them. Such a rule has to be reviewed by the whole choir; upon agreement, it should be forwarded to the overseer for vetting and to the resident pastor for approval.

5. Once a principle or rule is agreed upon, all are expected to comply with it afterward; no one shall be above the rule.

6. It is expected that every vessel of the Lord should be clean; every member of this choir is termed a worker, and as such, your life in church and outside counts. In the event of defiance according to scriptures, appropriate discipline shall be awarded, up to suspension or eventual removal from the choir ministry.

7. We serve a God of order and moderation; all choir apparel should be worn in a decent manner; no private areas should be revealed at any time. The choir director has the capacity to reprimand anyone that defies these instructions.

8. The choir body is one and should function as such; in the event of multiple services, all members of the choir are expected to function, and if any are unable to make it due to reasons beyond their control, appropriate permission should be obtained from the choir director.

9. The choir meeting holds every Saturday but is subject to change should any church program exist within that time frame.

10. The time schedule for the choir meeting will be as follows:

    1) Opening prayers - 10:00 - 10:05

    2) Exhortation - 10:05 - 10:15

3) Review of previous performances - 10:15 - 10:35

4) Rehearsal of special songs - 10:35 - 12:15

5) Rehearsal of praise & worship - 12:15 - 12:50

6) Closing & benediction - 12:50 - 01:00

11. Special numbers, praise, and worship renditions will be prepared on a monthly basis, in addition to the attire, by the choir director, forwarded to the overseer for approval before being posted on the platform.

12. The choir director is expected to be always prepared; in the event of the relevant preparedness of the ministers or other defiance, the choir director is expected to take over the ministration for that day or reassign it to another.

13. The office and ministry of the choir shall operate under this guide, with possible review in the future to ensure that this ministry is fulfilling its calling and blessing lives.

Decoration and Logistics Unit

To ensure the beautification of the church auditorium and to guarantee that all the supplies needed in the church are adequately provided.

Operations of this unit

1. This unit shall be responsible for the beautification of the church, from the altar to the main sanctuary.
2. It shall be responsible for purchasing, on a timely basis, toiletries, water, communion, and cleaning supplies.
3. The unit shall be responsible for recognizing brethren celebrating their birthdays. Birthday cards signed by the pastor will be sent out regularly.

4. The unit shall also ensure the accurate record-keeping of all purchases, donations, and general inventories.

Media and Publicity Unit:

The Media and Publicity Unit plays a crucial role in the church by managing various aspects of communication and technology to provide an engaging worship experience for both in-person and online audiences.

Operations of the Media and Publicity Unit

This unit shall ensure the following:

1. Proper connection and readiness of all audio equipment, which includes the usage of microphones, speakers, and instruments.
2. Proper connection and readiness of all video equipment and projections. Such tasks should be coordinated in a timely manner as it relates to the projection of scriptures, hymns, and other necessary projections as needed.
3. Proper representation of the church on all social media handles, which should be coordinated in a safe manner to protect the interests of the church, members, and viewers.
4. All church programs are to be projected live, except for some reserved instances as directed by the Resident Pastor.

DEFINITION OF TERMS IN THE LEADERSHIP/GENERAL CHURCH FORUM

1. An ordained leader is an individual who has completed the leadership school of training, graduated, and been ordained into the leadership body of the church. Ordained leaders can attend scheduled leadership meetings.
2. A worker is someone who has completed the Believers School of Ministry, graduated, and is actively serving in a department of their choice.
3. An overseer is a person selected to supervise the operations of a unit whose direct coordinator has not completed the leadership class. The overseer serves as the connecting link between the leadership body and the head of the specified unit.
4. The overseer is responsible for effectively communicating decisions from the leadership forum to the unit via the unit coordinator. Unit coordinators are allowed to manage the unit according to the guidelines provided in this operational manual. However, the overseer must monitor the overall operations periodically.
5. A member is an individual who has attended the church and completed the Believers School of Ministry.

LEADERSHIP OF SERVICE UNITS

A. Service Unit Executives

Each service unit shall be coordinated by an executive comprising the following:

1. Unit Leader
2. Assistant Unit Leader
3. Secretary

Where additional hands and offices are required, approval shall be obtained from the Resident Pastor.

B. Terms of Reference for the Executives of the Unit

1. Ensuring the fulfillment of the objectives of the unit.
2. General coordination of the unit.
3. Membership enlistment.
4. Maintaining discipline within the unit.
5. Ensuring membership welfare.
6. Liaising with other service units as may be necessary.
7. Reporting to the Assigned Leadership Board.
8. Shall serve for a period of two (2) years, renewable once.

C. Criteria for Nomination

1. Minimum of two-year church membership of the Local Assembly.
2. Where membership is less than two years, a letter must be produced from the previous local assembly and duly signed by the Resident Pastor after consultation with the Regional Pastor. Ordination is an added advantage.

3. Active unit membership participation.
4. Active departmental unit participation.
5. Believers School of Ministry attendance.
6. Stability of family life, if married.
7. Financial stability and integrity.
8. Tenure is two years and renewable only once.

D. Nomination Process

1. Membership of each unit shall be involved in the nomination and selection process.
2. Nomination and selection shall be done in a general meeting of the Unit.
3. Nomination shall be done by each member of the unit upon completing a printed form in confidentiality.
4. Pastors in the church shall be deployed to administer nomination/selection.
5. The list of selected unit leaders shall be ratified by the Pastors/Ministers Forum.
6. The list of ratified unit leaders shall be submitted to the Regional Pastor; once confirmed,
7. Pastors shall be assigned to introduce the newly selected leaders to their respective units at a general meeting.

E. Monitoring and Record-Keeping

1. Proper monitoring of service units is necessary.
2. Each unit should select an appropriate day of the week or month for their meetings.
3. The unit leader is responsible for maintaining records of names, attendance, contributions, and active engagement of all members within the unit.

4. Members of each unit should be encouraged by their leadership to forward observations and recommendations towards the enhancement of the unit's goals and objectives to the pastor or group leadership.
5. To ensure effectiveness, each unit will be equipped with the necessary resources.
6. It is recommended that any unit not actively contributing to the growth of the church should be dissolved.
7. Free-will offerings may be taken during service unit meetings, but all such offerings must be duly accounted for through the necessary accounting processes.

CENTRAL CHURCH APPOINTED POSITIONS

The Resident Pastor

The Resident Pastor shall be an individual who has gone through the school of ministry of the church, cleared from the headquarters, and ordained into the office of a Pastor. The resident pastor shall work in close proximity with the leadership of the church to ensure a smooth running of the Church of Christ.

Below are the qualities of the Resident Pastor:

1. Be born again
2. Be a man of one wife or a woman of one husband
3. Have his/her children under control
4. Have a testimony of good report among the brethren
5. Have gone through the relevant training in the church - Believers class, workers in training, leadership, and ministerial class
6. Be ordained in this church either by the General Overseer or Regional Pastor
7. Be able to communicate in an effective manner

The Resident Pastor shall be responsible for the following:

1. Be strong in the word and be able to communicate the same to other parishioners
2. Be strong in prayers and be able to demonstrate the same during services
3. Ensure to be in church on time, oversee the administration of all services, deliver a timely message according to the assigned outline

4. Be available to attend to the needs of the members via counseling
5. Ensure to collaborate with other leaders over any major decision to be made. Such a decision must be made only with the approval of the Regional Pastor or the General Overseer.
6. Regularly visit and check on the welfare of the members, and report any findings to the general leadership
7. The Resident Pastor serving in a full-time capacity may not be able to do any other employment. This position shall have service hours and office hours. Service hours shall be all the times for the regular church services. Office hours shall run from Monday to Friday, from 8 am to 5 pm.
8. The Resident full-time Pastor shall be on a monthly salary plus housing expense on an agreed amount from the Headquarters church
9. The Resident Pastor reserves the right to refuse all remunerations and housing expenses, but must be in full compliance with all responsibilities
10. The Resident Pastor must not lobby any member for money or be found to involve in any misconduct with any of his/her parishioners
11. The Resident Pastor shall rotate or may be transferred to another location after serving 2 years in the current location
12. The Resident Pastor shall be answerable to the Regional Pastor or Regional Coordinator

The Associate Pastor

An Associate Pastor is an individual that has followed due process and been ordained in this church (Divine Touch Bible Church). All the qualities expected of the Resident Pastor are also applicable to the Associate Pastor.

Responsibilities of the Associate Pastor:

1. The Associate Pastor shall serve in a supportive role to the Resident Pastor
2. The Associate Pastor assumes the role of the Resident Pastor in the event of non-availability
3. The Associate Pastor shall be free to take employment outside the church
4. The Associate Pastor shall not be under any remuneration from the church
5. The Associate Pastor can serve as the Youth or Children's Pastor
6. The Associate Pastor shall be answerable to the Resident Pastor
7. All forms of misconduct shall be avoided; the Associate Pastor must always live in holiness and purity

The Evangelist

The Evangelist is an individual who has been trained, observed, and ordained into the office of an evangelist.

Responsibilities of an Evangelist:

1. The Evangelist will serve in a supportive role to the Resident Pastor.
2. The Evangelist will ensure aggressive soul-winning on a weekly, monthly, and annual basis.
3. The Evangelist shall strategize on a regular basis, creating various outlets for evangelism and engaging the whole church.
4. The Evangelist shall ensure that all programs in the church are well-planned and geared towards soul-winning.

5. The Evangelist shall collaborate with the zonal coordinator, Associate Pastor, and the Resident Pastor on all matters relating to newly won souls.
6. The Evangelist shall not be full-time; this individual is permitted to seek outside employment, provided it does not interfere with church engagements and activities.
7. The Evangelist must not engage in any form of misconduct with members and must live a chaste, holy, and disciplined life.

Deacon and Deaconesses

These brethren shall be selected via recommendation from the church and approved by the Resident Pastor with the help of the Holy Spirit. The deacon and deaconesses shall have the same qualities as the Resident and Associate Pastor.

Responsibilities of the deacon and deaconess:

1. Serve in a supportive role to the ordained ministers, ensuring all necessary support is available.
2. Regularly moderate the service, teach the word, or exhort the brethren.
3. Be able to moderate a covenant naming event and other invitations that the resident pastor cannot fulfill via appointment.
4. Ensure that all departments and units run smoothly.
5. Ensure that members are well-served during programs.
6. Ensure that aggrieved members are well-managed and that issues are resolved in a timely manner.
7. Provide support for the Resident Pastor during programs.
8. Serve in a supportive role to the Evangelist to ensure that all soul-winning programs are well-managed.

9. Ensure that the church is open on time for all service days and that all doors are locked and equipment secured on off-service days.
10. Be answerable to the Resident Pastor, Regional Pastor, or Regional Coordinator.

The Zonal Coordinators

These brethren shall be carefully selected by the Resident Pastor.

The duties of the zonal coordinators are as follows:

1. Be assigned to a zone and ensure to capture the names and phone numbers of all members in the assigned zone.
2. Assigned zones may be different from the original location of the coordinator.
3. Each coordinator is expected to connect with all members in their zone to familiarize themselves.
4. Zonal coordinators are to ensure that assigned members always attend church services.
5. At the end of Sunday service, each coordinator is to conduct a personal roll call. If any members are absent, calls should be made, and a report should be delivered to the assigned platform at the end of that particular Sunday.
6. No private visitation is encouraged; if any of the members desire a visit, please refer to the hospitality group and inform the resident pastor.
7. As much as possible, each coordinator is to ensure the avoidance of any form of misconduct, mismanagement, and disorderly behavior.
8. Gross misconduct, such as merchandising, financial exchange, and any activity outside of the assigned description, should be avoided.

9. Timely reports per Sunday are required and should be placed in the assigned platform, including information on what transpired, your intervention, and how it was handled.
10. The zonal coordinator shall collaborate with the Resident Pastors, Evangelist, and the hospitality team.
11. The zonal coordinator shall be answerable to the Resident Pastor, Regional Pastor, or Regional Coordinator.

General Secretary

The General Secretary shall be appointed by the Resident Pastor, and the following responsibilities apply:

1. Capturing a complete database of all members, which includes names, current addresses, phone numbers, and next of kin's information.
2. Ensuring the capture of all testimonies shared in the church during all services.
3. Ensuring the capture of minutes from all meetings at all levels.
4. Being responsible for fixing, canceling, and arranging all appointments with the Resident Pastor.
5. Ensuring the collation and coordination of end-of-year reports from all units and departments, and being ready to present them to the church.
6. Ensuring the presentation of letters to all financial donors, detailing the total in cash or non-cash values, at the end of the fiscal year.
7. The General Secretary shall be answerable to the Resident Pastor, Associate, or the Regional Pastor/Coordinator.

Assistant General Secretary

This individual shall be appointed by the Resident Pastor and shall serve as an assistant to the General Secretary. This person assumes the role of General Secretary when they are not available.

Financial Secretary

The Financial Secretary shall be appointed by the Resident Pastor and shall be responsible for the following:

1. Total count and collation of all financial contributions to the church per service.
2. Ensuring the deposit of funds into an assigned church account within 48 hours of collection.
3. If a deposit cannot be completed within the assigned time, the Resident Pastor should be made aware.
4. Ensuring the collation of total financial contributions on a monthly basis and forwarding them to the Resident Pastor, Regional Coordinator, or Regional Pastor.
5. Ensuring timely reporting of any donation in check form that exceeds $2,000 from an unknown donor.
6. Ensuring the reporting of any bounced checks or financial irregularities to the appropriate authorities.
7. Being answerable to the Resident Pastor or Regional Pastor.

Assistant Financial Secretary

The Assistant Financial Secretary shall be appointed by the Resident Pastor and shall serve in a supportive role to the Financial Secretary.

REGIONAL LEVEL

The church shall operate at both a branch and regional level in the diaspora. The following positions shall be appointed at the regional level, and these positions shall supersede individual branches.

Office of Directors:

Director of Programs –

Responsible for all the events of the year, in charge of the major programs of the year. This position entails the following responsibilities:

1. Securing the date for the main meetings of the month and year.
2. Securing all venues ahead of the events.
3. Mobilizing all logistics to and from the event center.
4. Accounting for all inventories of all programs.
5. Working within the budget assigned to all programs.
6. Creating sub-units to facilitate the flow of any programs of the year.
7. Submitting timely reports after any program, including progress, challenges encountered, recommendations, financial reports, etc.
8. Working with individual units or departments in charge of any programs for the year.
9. Ensuring preparations are made ahead of time for any programs and advising the church on the mode of operations.
10. Reporting to the Regional Pastor.
11. Generating and maintaining appropriate records.

Director of Internal Operations –

Responsible for week-to-week engagement, including but not limited to:

1. Ensuring all services are well prepared, including Wednesday, Sunday, and special services.
2. Ensuring that the church is open and closed on a timely basis.
3. Managing the week-to-week inventory of all church materials and making appropriate requests for timely purchases.
4. Overseeing all internal operations, including altar preparation/maintenance and maintaining decorum during all services.
5. Liaising with all appropriate units that function in all services, ensuring adequate preparation prior to services and special events.
6. Ensuring special guests and visitors during all services are well maintained, managed, and blessed.
7. Accounting for and storing all proceeds from Thanksgiving events in designated areas.
8. Collaborating with appropriate units and departments to ensure all first-time visitors and guests during special programs are well received, addressed, and followed up on.
9. Attending departmental meetings as needed to ensure all weekly meetings are well managed and challenges are addressed in a timely manner.
10. Reporting to the Regional Pastor.
11. Generating and maintaining appropriate records.

Director of Welfare –

Tasked with the following responsibilities, reflecting the belief that Jesus cares for the people, and as such, every church of Christ should extend care to its members:

1. Ensuring week-to-week numerical statistics are captured.

2. Ensuring appropriate follow-ups are done on all members absent from service more than two services in a month.
3. Ensuring the appropriate unit assigned to manage the welfare of the sick and newborns are performing their duties.
4. Serving as the zonal director in charge of all zonal coordinators, occasionally liaising with them to ensure all members are well captured, followed up on, and providing timely intervention if needed.
5. Assigning new members to zones and the zonal coordinator in charge.
6. Supplying information on all members' concerns and health challenges to the Resident Pastor as soon as possible.
7. Ensuring that all leaders, ministers, and assigned workers are well taken care of during all programs.
8. Liaising with the appropriate department to ensure no one feels left behind or abandoned.
9. Being flexible to cover up for any zonal coordinator inactive due to family concerns or unexpected emergencies.
10. Ensuring all first-time visitors are followed up on until they are established in the faith.
11. Reporting to the Regional Pastor.
12. Generating and maintaining appropriate records for all welfare-related activities.

Director of Financial Services –

As a well-established and approved 501c3 religious organization, the Office of the Director of Financial Services (D.O.F.S) shall be responsible for the following:

1. Ensuring that all envelopes are available during all services and available for distribution on demand.
2. Ensuring the offering box is well placed and available on demand.

3. Ensuring that all monies in cash, check, or online are well accounted for, and deposits are made within 48 hours of collections.
4. Ensure that all verifiable and approved expenses are well documented with date, purpose of purchase, and mode of transfer.
5. Ensure that an appropriate record of account on an annual basis is made available on demand from the headquarters church, IRS, or the Resident Pastor.
6. Shall ensure that the church spending per month does not exceed, on a maximum level, 45% of its monthly earnings.
7. Shall ensure that a financial report is made available to the leaders and the general church on an annual basis.
8. Shall be answerable on demand to the IRS, interested public officials, the headquarters church, the resident pastor, the leaders, and the church in general.
9. Shall not approve any spending above $1k without the approval of the resident Pastor.
10. Shall also report on a timely basis any single donation that is above $2,000 to the resident Pastor immediately.
11. Shall ensure that the monthly, quarterly, and annual tithe of the church is paid to the appropriate quarter.
12. The office of the D.O.F.S shall report to the Regional Pastor.
13. Appropriate records shall be generated and kept per time.

Director of Outreach –

The ministry of Jesus is characterized by constant outreach to the poor, less privileged, the unreached, and the orphans.

The office of the Director of Outreach shall be responsible for the following:

1. Ensuring that community engagement programs are well managed.

2. Shall be responsible for reaching out to the poor, less privileged, and the orphans at the end of every quarter fasting and prayers. Countries well represented in the church should be mostly attended to in consideration of the resources or finances collected.

3. Shall ensure that the weekly, monthly, and annual evangelism outreaches are well managed.

4. Shall be responsible for the printing of all flyers and banners of events, and ensure that they are all properly shared.

5. Mobilize all members in active participation in all evangelistic events.

6. Shall be responsible for purchases, budgeting, and execution of all the needful for outreach events.

7. Shall be responsible for the publicity of all major programs of the church, both on the ground and online, in a timely basis.

8. Shall also ensure that all evangelistic materials and resources for outreach are available in a timely manner.

9. Shall also engage in innovative ideas for church growth via various approved scriptural means.

10. Shall, in a timely basis, liaise with the Resident Pastor on the next outreach, church growth initiatives, etc.

11. The office of the D.O.F.S shall report to the Regional Pastor.

12. Appropriate records shall be generated and kept per time.

FOUNDATION OF OUR FAITH

Every visitor is a potential member, and as such, all intending visitors who aspire to become members will be required to go through a 6-week Believers Foundational Teaching. Details of the teachings are outlined below.

School of Ministry:

Believers Foundation Class

1. Basic Bible Hermeneutics/Rudiments of Salvation
2. Sanctification Experience
3. Justification by Faith
4. Sanctification
5. Prayers
6. Scriptural Giving
7. Baptism
8. Communion
9. Statement of Faith

Workers in Training

1. Doctrine Part 1
2. Word Foundation
3. Stewardship
4. Dynamics of Holiness
5. Prayer
6. Spiritual Gift

Leadership Training

1. Leadership

2. Doctrine 2
3. New Creation Realities
4. Evangelism
5. Church Administration

Minister in Training

1. Theology Part 1
2. Theology Part 2
3. Biblical Business Concept
4. Pentateuch
5. Eschatology
6. Hermeneutics

LESSON 1

Topic: Basic Bible Hermeneutics

The Bible remains our main standard of practice in this commission. All scriptures, instructions, disciplines, and purposes shall be rooted in the Bible. God's word, according to 2 Cor. 3:16, clearly states that Bible means Basic Instruction Before Leaving Earth. I believe this is very true, as all that is needed for life and godliness have been inscribed on the pages of the scriptures (2 Peter 1:1-4).

There are many versions of the Holy Bible. In this commission, we base most of our teachings and quotations on the King James Version Bible. The Bible comprises 66 books: 39 books from the Old Testament and 27 books from the New Testament. It is essential to familiarize yourself with the locations of each book and its purpose for easy studying.

The layout is as follows:

1. The Pentateuch – Genesis, Exodus, Leviticus, Numbers, Deuteronomy

2. The Historical Books – Joshua, Judges, Ruth, First and Second Samuel, First and Second Kings, First and Second Chronicles, Ezra, Nehemiah, and Esther

3. The Wisdom Books – Job, Psalms, Proverbs, Ecclesiastes, Song of Solomon

4. The Major Prophets – Isaiah, Jeremiah, Lamentations, Ezekiel, Daniel

5. The Minor Prophets – Hosea, Joel, Amos, Obadiah, Jonah, Micah, Nahum, Habakkuk, Zephaniah, Haggai, Zechariah, Malachi

6. The Gospels – Matthew, Mark, Luke, John
7. The History of the Early Church – Acts
8. The Pauline Epistles – Romans, First and Second Corinthians, Galatians, Ephesians, Philippians, Colossians, First and Second Thessalonians, First and Second Timothy, Titus, Philemon
9. The General Epistles – Hebrews, James, First and Second Peter, First, Second, and Third John, Jude
10. The Apocalypse – Revelation

Words of Wisdom:

1. Endeavor to study one chapter of the Bible daily; studying books by books has been proven to be effective.
2. Try to memorize one scripture of interest daily, as this will build you up spiritually.
3. Have a journal where you write what you gain from the chapter you study and any possible questions that you have.
4. Pray that the Lord will give you understanding of what you have read through the power of the Holy Spirit.

LESSON 2

Topic: Salvation

Salvation Defined

Salvation refers to the act of God's grace in delivering His people from bondage to sin and condemnation, transferring them to the kingdom of His beloved Son [Col. 1:13], and giving them eternal life [Romans 6:23] all on the basis of what Christ accomplished in His atoning sacrifice. The Bible says we are saved by grace through faith, and that not of ourselves; it is the gift of God [Ephesians 2:8]. Emphasis is not on what we have done, but because of what He has done – Romans 5:8.

Purpose of Salvation

The purpose of salvation is rooted in its Greek meaning. The study of salvation is called soteriology, from the Greek word "Soteria," meaning "salvation." This term is virtually synonymous with the overall concept of redemption and includes a past, present, and future sense. As Christians, we were saved from the penalty of sin when God brought us to faith in Christ. Romans 3:23 declares, "All have sinned and come short of the glory of the Lord." The sinning man needs a delivering savior, and in John 3:16, God's gift was manifested in Jesus Christ so that whosoever believes in Him will not perish but have eternal life. When you come to Christ, you receive God's kind of life, "ZOE," which extends from this life to the life beyond this life.

How Can I Be Saved?

1. Acts 4:12 – Salvation is in the name of Jesus.
2. Revelation 3:20 – Jesus is standing at the door of your heart, and if you confess with your mouth, you shall be saved.

3. Romans 10:7-10 – When you believe in your heart and confess with your mouth, you shall be saved.
4. Acts 16:13 – There is no other way than believing in the Lord Jesus Christ.
5. John 14:6 – It is not a way; He is the way to salvation and being saved.

Maintaining Your Salvation Experience

1. Study the Bible – 2 Timothy 2:15
2. Locate a Bible-believing church – Hebrews 10:25
3. Find and belong to a small Bible study group – John 5:39
4. Share your faith with your friends and loved ones.

Results of Salvation

Adoption, Sanctification, Resurrection, Heaven, Beatific Vision, and Glorification.

LESSON 3:

Topic: Justification

Justification by Faith

Text: Romans 5:1-10, Romans 1:17, Romans 3:28, Romans 4:5, Romans 4:22-25, Romans 5:19, Romans 8:33, 1 Corinthians 1:30, 1 Corinthians 6:17, Galatians 2:18, Philippians 3:9, Galatians 3:27, and Colossians 1:27.

What is Justification? Justification in Christian theology is God's act of removing the guilt and penalty of sin while at the same time declaring a sinner righteous through Christ's atoning sacrifice. "If when we were enemies, we were reconciled to God through the death of His Son, much more, having been reconciled, we shall be saved by His life" - Romans 5:10.

In biblical terms, justification is a divine verdict of "not guilty—fully righteous." It is the reversal of God's attitude toward the sinner. Whereas He formerly condemned, He now vindicates. Although the sinner once lived under God's wrath, as a believer, he or she is now under God's blessing.

Justification is more than simple pardon; pardon alone would still leave the sinner without merit before God. So, when God justifies, He imputes divine righteousness to the sinner (Romans 4:22-25). Christ's own infinite merit thus becomes the ground on which the believer stands before God (Romans 5:19, 1 Corinthians 1:30, Philippians 3:9). Justification elevates the believer to a realm of full acceptance and divine privilege in Jesus Christ.

Therefore, because of justification, believers not only are perfectly free from any charge of guilt (Romans 8:33) but also have the full merit of Christ reckoned to their personal account (Romans 5:17).

Here are the forensic realities that flow out of justification:

- We are adopted as sons and daughters (Romans 8:15)
- We become fellow-heirs with Christ (Romans 8:17)
- We are united with Christ so that we become one with Him (1 Corinthians 6:17)
- We are henceforth "in Christ" (Galatians 3:27) and He in us (Colossians 1:27)

How Justification and Sanctification Differ

Justification is distinct from sanctification because in justification God does not make the sinner righteous; He declares that person righteous (Romans 3:28, Galatians 2:16).

Notice how justification and sanctification are distinct from one another:

- Justification imputes Christ's righteousness to the sinner's account (Romans 6:1-7; 8:11-14)
- Justification takes place outside sinners and changes their standing (Romans 5:1-2); sanctification is internal and changes the believer's state (Romans 6:19)
- Justification is an event; sanctification is a process.
- Key Scriptures: Romans 5:1; assigned reading: Romans Chapters 6 and 7.

LESSON 4

Topic: Sanctification

TEXT: I Thes 4:2; I Thes 5:20-23; John 17:15-17, II Tim 2:21, II Thes 2:14; Romans 6:6, Heb 13:12; I Cor 6:11; Heb 10:14, Exodus 31:13.

Sanctification Defined

Sanctification, or in its verbal form, sanctify, literally means "to set apart" for special use or purpose, that is, to make holy or sacred. Therefore, sanctification refers to the state or process of being set apart, i.e., made holy. In Christianity, the term can be used to refer to objects which are set apart for special purposes, but the most common use within Christian theology is in reference to the change brought about by God in a believer, begun at the point of salvation or justification and continuing throughout the life of the believer. II Cor 6:17.

Process of Sanctification

According to I Thes 4:3; it is the will of God for us to be sanctified, so when we surrender our lives to the Lord Jesus Christ, the process of sanctification is initiated within us. The agents of sanctification that will be unveiled underneath are to be deployed by believers in order to appropriate the full benefit of sanctification. He wants us to be holy but there is an expectation that must be fulfilled by the believer for holiness to be perfected. The concept of sanctification is tied closely to Grace, and the term is usually reserved for reference to people rather than objects. Following a reading of the doctrine of the perseverance of the saints, the word "sanctified" can be used as a shorthand for "born again" in the sense of "set apart by God." Unwanted habits and character are being dealt with in the process of sanctification.

Agent of Sanctification

- God himself as the sanctifier - Exodus 31:13
- Jesus Christ purifies us by his blood - I John 1:7-10
- The Holy Spirit burns every impurity with an unquenchable fire - Matthew 3:12
- The word of God - John 17:17
- Our conscious effort - II Cor 6:17; I Thes 5:23

Maintaining Sanctification Experience

- **STUDYING THE WORD OF GOD**
    - Leviticus 11:44 "...consecrate yourselves therefore, and be holy, for I am holy…"
    - Matthew 5:48 "...you therefore must be perfect, as your heavenly Father is perfect…"
    - Romans 6:22 "...but now that you have been set free from sin and have become slaves of God, the fruit you get leads to sanctification and its end, eternal life."
    - I Corinthians 6:11 "...but you were washed, you were sanctified, you were justified in the name of the Lord Jesus Christ and by the spirit of our God."
    - 2 Corinthians 3:18 "and we all, with veiled face, beholding the glory of the Lord, are being transformed into the same image from one degree of glory to another. For this comes from the Lord who is the spirit."
    - 2 Corinthians 7:1 "...beloved, let us cleanse ourselves from every defilement of body and spirit, bringing holiness to completion in the fear of God."
- **PRAYERS** - John 17:17
- **DECISION** - I Thessalonians 5:23; I Peter 1:15-16
- **FELLOWSHIP** - Proverbs 27:17; Hebrews 10:25

LESSON 5

Topic: Prayers

Text: Matt 6:9-13; Matt 7:7-11; Mark 11:24-25

What is Prayer?

Prayer is the act of communing with God. It is not a monologue conversation but a dialogue, and as such, requires the whole heart if we are to receive answers to prayers. Prayer is the only connection between humanity and divinity; our heart relates to His when we pray in accordance with scriptures. As I will always say, prayer moves the hand that moves the world. If you want to experience change and divine encounter, you must generate a strong appetite for prayers.

Jesus, the Lord of glory, prayed in order to accomplish a successful ministry here on earth. It is not a recommendation but a requirement for an effective Christian life. For us to learn His plans for our lives, we need to talk to Him in the place of prayers; God wants to hear from us.

Elements of Effective Prayer

There are vital scriptural elements that guarantee effective prayers:

1. The name of Jesus - we are expected to pray to the Father in the name of Jesus (John 14:13-14)

2. Pray with the word of God (Psalms 138:2)

3. Pray with faith (Matt 21:21-23)

Acts of Prayers

How do we pray? This was the same question the disciples asked Jesus. Jesus responded to their request in Matthew chapter 7. From this scripture, the acts of prayers are developed:

1. A - Acknowledgment of His worth and works in your life (Psalms 48:1-7)
2. C - Confess your shortcomings and transgressions to Him (1 John 1:7-10)
3. T - Thanking Him for what He has done and for what He will do (Psalms 89:1; Psalms 34:1; Psalms 103: 1-5)
4. S - Supplication and request (John 14:12-16)

Boosting Your Prayer Life

To develop and boost your prayer life, the following factors must be in place:

1. Pray with the assistance of the Holy Spirit (Rom 8:26)
2. Pray with forgiveness and love (Mark 11:25)
3. Pray and fast occasionally as led and instructed by the Spirit of the Lord (Matt 17:21)
4. Start your prayers with praise and worship
5. Be consistent, faithful, and dedicated in order to maintain a consistent and growing prayer life.

LESSON 6

Topic: Scriptural Giving

Text: Gen 4:1-10, Ii Cor 9:5-8, Luke 6:38, Psalms 126:5-6, Proverbs 11:24-26

What is Scriptural Giving?

Scriptural giving involves freely transferring the possession of something to another in the name of the Lord or causing or allowing someone or something to have something. When we give in the name of the Lord, it must be love-motivated, or our reward becomes hindered (I Cor 13:1-4).

Types of Giving

1. Offering - Basic (Deut 16:17), Thanksgiving, Sacrificial (Gen 22:1-19)
2. Tithe - Mal 3:7-10 (Your tithe is the 10% of your increase)
3. Covenant seed - Psalms 50:4-6
4. First fruit - Proverbs 3:9-10

Why Should We Give?

1. I give because God has given to me - James 1:17, Eph 1:3, I Tim 6:17
2. I give because I want to please God - II Cor 9:13, Matt 6:21
3. I want to lay up treasures in heaven - Matt 6:4, I Tim 6:19
4. I want to be a compassionate person - I John 3:17, James 2:15-16
5. I want to be a worshipper of God. Giving is a sacrifice that pleases God - Phil 4:18, Heb 13:16

Who Should We Give to?

1. Give to God through the Church - Mal 3:7-10
2. Give to the poor - Matt 41:1-5
3. Give to ministries that are involved in mission work - Zech 1:17-23

Conditions of Giving

There are basic scriptural principles that should guide our giving life if our offerings are to be acceptable.

1. I should give in a pre-planned, systematic way - I Cor 16:2, 2 Cor 9:7
2. I should give in secret to the Lord, not in public before men - Matt 6:1-4
3. I should give sacrificially at times - II Cor 8:2-3
4. I should give willingly - II Cor 8:12
5. I should give bountifully, not sparingly - II Cor 9:6-7

Blessings of Obedience

1. I and my family will be blessed. God blesses faith and obedience, which are at the heart of Biblical giving. If you give, God promises to supply your needs - Phil 4:17-19
2. Others' needs will be met - Phil 4:16, 18; 2 Cor 8:13-14; 9-12. God's work and workers will not be hindered. The needs of the poor will be met.
3. God will be thanked and glorified - 2 Cor 9:11-13,15. He will get the praise if we give His way.
4. The body of Christ will be united in prayer and fellowship - 2 Cor 9:14. Since your heart follows your treasure, you will be concerned about and will pray for those to whom you give.

5. People will spend eternity with God because of your giving. How can you put a price tag on that? What could possibly be more important? -Matt 25:21-46

LESSON 7

Topic: Baptism

Text: *Romans 6:1-11, Matthew 3:13-17*

What is Baptism?

Baptism is a divine act that is endorsed in the scriptures and serves as an outward confirmation of an inner renewal. When you have given your life to Jesus Christ, you then follow His bidding and His commands (Matthew 28:18-20).

Water Baptism

Many people ask if it is required for salvation. Baptism isn't an act that gets us into heaven; it is faith in Jesus Christ as Savior and Lord that offers that assurance. Baptism (by full immersion as taught in the Bible) is an act of obedience that should be an immediate part of our acceptance of the gift of grace offered by Jesus Christ.

However, this does not mean that someone who truly gives their heart to Jesus on a deathbed, in the heat of warfare, or in a crashing airplane will be kept out of heaven because they failed to be baptized. The thief on the cross next to Jesus didn't have time to be baptized before he died, but he had an opportunity to believe in Jesus and put his trust in Him. Jesus responded by saying, "Assuredly, I say to you, today you will be with me in Paradise" (Luke 23:43).

True faith in Jesus Christ and His work on the cross for our sins is sufficient for salvation. Christ has already done everything. His grace doesn't require any additional "works" by us. With that understanding, Jesus Christ commands us to be baptized (Matthew 28:18-20), and therefore, all believers should be baptized. Immediately following Christ's command, the Book of Acts describes the practice of administering baptism to almost every group or individual who believed in the preaching of the gospel by the apostles (Acts 2:37-41; 8:5-13; 8:35-39; 9:10-18; 10:34-48; 16:13-15; 16:30-33; 18:8; and 19:1-6).

Significance of Water Baptism

According to the Bible, the symbolism of baptism declares that three things happen to believers who are baptized:

1. They die with Christ to their old self.

2. They rise with Christ to become a new creature.

3. They are incorporated in their new life with a living community that looks for the coming of the Lord (Romans 6:1-11).

DTBC Doctrine on Baptism

1. Be of an accountable age, being able to discern evil from wrong. According to John 3:1-10, we don't baptize infants.

2. Accept Jesus Christ into your life as Lord and Savior (Mark 16:15-16).

3. Attend a baptismal class for in-depth teaching and be ready for baptism when the church calls for it.

4. Immersion baptism - the church doesn't sprinkle water on people's faces or heads; you are dipped inside water, fully immersed, which symbolizes His death, and you are completely lifted, which symbolizes His resurrection (Romans 6:4-5).

5. Live a newness of life afterward (Romans 6:8-10).

6. Key scripture: Matthew 28:19

LESSON 8

Topic: Communion

Text: John 6:30-55; Luke 22:18-25; 1 Cor 11:17-34

What is Communion?

The service of Christian worship at which bread and wine are consecrated and shared, communion uses bread as a symbol for the body of Jesus and wine as a symbol for the blood of Christ. Most Christian organizations call it Holy Communion, Eucharist, Lord's Supper, etc. The most significant aspect, regardless of the differences in names, is what it carries and its importance in the life of a believer. Holy Communion uses bread as a symbol of Jesus' body and wine as a symbol of his blood. The act of taking communion does not save us; it is an act of worship and remembrance.

Where Did Communion Come From?

Jesus started the tradition of communion. He instructed his followers to use bread and wine to remember the sacrifice He was going to make when He died for our sins on the cross (1 Cor 11:23-26). Jesus called Himself "the bread of life," which means we are nourished by Him, we survive because of Him, and He satisfies us when everything else leaves us empty (John 6:48-51). There is a connection between our nearness to Jesus, believing in Him, and being fulfilled by Him (John 6:35). The early Church celebrated Jesus by taking communion, sometimes every day (Acts 2:42-44). They saw that every time they gathered around a table to eat and drink, it was a chance to recognize Jesus and thank God for all He has done.

Significance of the Communion

It was during the age-old celebration of the Passover on the eve of His death that Jesus instituted a significant new fellowship meal that we observe to this day. It is an integral part of Christian worship. It causes us to remember our Lord's death and resurrection and to look for His glorious return in the future. During the Last Supper, a Passover celebration, Jesus took a loaf of bread and gave thanks to God. As He broke it and gave it to His disciples, He said, "This is my body given for you; do this in remembrance of me". In the same way, after the supper, He took the cup, saying, "This cup is the new covenant in my blood, which is poured out for you" (Luke 22:19-21).

Preparations

The accounts of the Lord's Supper are found in the Gospels (Matthew 26:26-29; Mark 14:17-25; Luke 22:7-22; and John 13:21-30). The apostle Paul wrote concerning the Lord's Supper in 1 Corinthians 11:23-29. Paul includes a statement not found in the Gospels: *"Therefore, whoever eats the bread or drinks the cup of the Lord in an unworthy manner will be guilty of sinning against the body and blood of the Lord. A man ought to examine himself before he eats of the bread and drinks of the cup. For anyone who eats and drinks without recognizing the body of the Lord eats and drinks judgment on himself"* (1 Corinthians 11:27-29).

We may ask what it means to partake of the bread and the cup "in an unworthy manner." It may mean to disregard the true meaning of the bread and the cup and to forget the tremendous price our Savior paid for our salvation. Or it may mean to allow the ceremony to become a dead and formal ritual or to come to the Lord's Supper with unconfessed sin. In keeping with Paul's instruction, we should examine ourselves before eating the bread and drinking the cup.

How Often Should We Observe the Lord's Table? (1 Corinthians 11:23-26) Often?

The bread that Jesus broke represents His body that was broken on the cross for us. The cup represents the blood He shed on our behalf, sealing a covenant between Him and us. Each time we observe the ordinance of communion, we are not only remembering what He did for us, but we are showing it as well to all who watch and all who participate. Communion is a beautiful picture of what happened at the cross, what it means, and how it impacts our lives as believers.

Since we take the Lord's Supper to remember Christ's death, we should take it fairly often. Some churches have a monthly Lord's Supper service; others do it bi-monthly; others weekly. Since the Bible does not give us specific instruction as to frequency, there is some latitude in how often a church should observe the Lord's Supper. It should be often enough to renew focus on Christ, without being so often that it becomes routine.

In any case, it is not the frequency that matters but the heart attitude of those who participate. We should partake with reverence, love, and a deep sense of gratitude for the Lord Jesus, who was willing to die on the cross to take upon Himself our sins.

Administration of Communion

1. Scriptures - 1 Cor 11:23-30 - shall be read.
2. Procedure - Post reading of the assigned verse.

The leading pastor shall ensure the following:

1. All congregants have the communion in their hands.
2. All congregants can open the communion with the bread and wine available.

3. The leading Pastor shall then pray for the bread and convert it into the flesh of Christ. Afterwards, the wine will be prayed for and converted into the blood of Jesus Christ.
4. The leading pastor shall direct the congregants to eat the flesh first, then followed by the wine.

LESSON 9: STATEMENT OF FAITH

We believe in, and live by, God the Father Almighty, maker of Heaven and Earth, and in Jesus Christ, His Son, and our Lord who was conceived by the Holy Ghost through the Word of God and born of the Virgin Mary. He suffered under Pontius Pilate, was crucified, dead, and buried. He descended into Hell, and He stripped Satan of his power. Upon the third day, He rose again and ascended into Heaven, where He is seated at the right hand of God the Father Almighty. We believe in the Holy Ghost, the worldwide body of Christ (His Church), the forgiveness of all sins, the resurrection of the dead, the communion of the saints, and life everlasting. We believe that through a profession of faith (trust) in the shed blood of Jesus Christ, His death, burial, resurrection, and ascension, one may become a partaker of their inheritance in Him.

1. We believe that the Bible is the inspired Word of God, written by holy men as they were instructed by God. It is the inherent Word of God (II Tim 3:16).

2. We believe that man was created good and upright, for God said, "Let us make man in our own image, after our likeness." But man voluntarily transgressed against God, and God has provided man with his only hope of salvation and redemption, which is in Jesus Christ, the Son of God (Gen 1:26-31; 3:17; Rom 5:12-21).

3. We believe that Jesus came as a man, was born of a virgin, and His father is God. We believe that Jesus was born without the inherited sin of Adam and, during his entire life, committed no sin. Jesus was the eternal Father made visible, apart from whom there is no God (I Tim 3:16; John 10:30; Isaiah 9:6; Luke 2:11; Rev 1:8).

4. We believe in the personal salvation of believers through the confession of sins, recognizing that Jesus Christ is the substitute for our sins, through his shed blood. It is by the grace of God, through faith in Jesus Christ and His shed blood, that we become an heir of God (Rom 10:9,10; I John 1:9; Eph 2: 8-9).

5. We believe that the new birth is a direct witness of the Spirit and is an inward confession of Jesus Christ (Rom 8:16). We believe that following salvation through Jesus Christ, you should be baptized, as commanded by the Lord Jesus. This was the command He left His apostles: "Go ye therefore, and teach all nations, baptizing them, in the name of the Father, and the Son, and the Holy Ghost" (Matt 28:19). Mark 16:16 reads, "He that believeth, and is baptized, shall be saved…"

6. We believe in divine healing through faith and that healing is a benefit of the atonement.

7. We believe in the nine gifts of the Holy Spirit and that these gifts are given throughout the Body of Christ and are in operation today (I Cor 12).

8. We believe in the imminent return, second coming of our Lord Jesus Christ for His Church (His Bride).

9. We believe that there is heaven and hell. Heaven is a place of eternal rest for the righteous (those who have accepted Jesus Christ as atonement for their sins), and hell is a place of eternal damnation for the unrighteous (those who do not accept Jesus Christ as their Lord and Savior) (Matt 28:19; Mark 16:16).

10. We believe in the millennial reign of Jesus, the revelation of the Lord Jesus Christ from heaven, and the millennial reign of Christ and his followers on earth (II Thes 1:7; Rom 11:26-27; Rev 20:1-7).

11. We believe in the Great Commission, to minister God's saving grace and to reach out to the poor and lost in spirit (Mark 16:15). And foremost, to honor and obey God's command, "Take the Gospel into all the world."

THE ORDINANCE OF WATER BAPTISM

What is Baptism?

Baptism is a divine act endorsed in the scriptures, and it is an outward confirmation of an inner renewal. When you have given your life to Jesus Christ, you then do his bidding and his commands (Matthew 28:18-20).

Water Baptism - Is it required for salvation?

Baptism isn't an act that gets us into heaven. It is faith in Jesus Christ as Savior and Lord that offers that assurance. Baptism (by full immersion as taught in the Bible) is an act of obedience that should be an immediate part of our acceptance of the gift of grace offered by Jesus Christ. However, it does not mean that one who truly gives their heart to Jesus on a death bed, in the heat of warfare, or in a crashing airplane, will be kept out of heaven because they failed to be baptized. The thief on the cross next to Jesus didn't have time to be baptized before he died, but he had an opportunity to believe in Jesus and put his trust in Him, and Jesus responded by saying, "Assuredly, I say to you, today you will be with me in Paradise" (Luke 23:43).

True faith in Jesus Christ and His work on the cross for our sins is sufficient for salvation. Christ has already done everything. His grace doesn't require any additional "works" by us. With that understanding, Jesus Christ commands us to be baptized (Matthew 28:18-20), and therefore, all believers should be baptized. Immediately following Christ's command, the Book of Acts describes the practice of administering baptism to almost every group or individual who believed in the preaching of the gospel by the apostles (Acts 2:37-41; 8:5-13; 8:35-39; 9:10-18; 10:34-48; 16:13-15; 16:30-33; 18:8; and 19:1-6).

Significance of Water Baptism

According to the Bible, the symbolism of baptism declares that three things happen to believers who are baptized:

1. They die with Christ to their old self.

2. They rise with Christ to become a new creature.

3. They are incorporated into their new life with a living community that looks for the coming of the Lord (Romans 6:1-11).

DTBC Doctrine on Baptism

1. Be of an accountable age, being able to discern evil from wrong. John 3:1-10, we don't baptize infants.

2. Accept Jesus Christ into your life as Lord and Savior. Mark 16:15-16.

3. Attend baptismal class for in-depth teaching and be ready for baptism when the church calls for it.

4. Immersion baptism - the church doesn't sprinkle water on people's faces or heads; you are dipped inside water, all immersed, which symbolizes his death, and you are completely lifted, which symbolizes his resurrection (Rom 6:4-5).

5. Live a newness of life afterward (Rom 6:8-10).

Administration of Baptism

From the New Testament enumeration of water baptism, the procedure is by complete immersion in water (Matt. 3:16; Rom. 6:3-4; Col. 2:12). Therefore, the water for baptism must be deep enough to fully submerge the person to be baptized. The following steps are required for the exercise of water baptism:

1. The people to be baptized must be born again.

2. The brethren are given a short exhortation on the scriptural mandate of water baptism and the associated blessing to provoke the faith of the

3. Altar call shall be made after the exhortation in case there are brethren who may need to rededicate their lives to Christ.

4. The brethren shall be led in prayers of expectation.

5. At the poolside, the Senior Pastor sanctifies the water by praying over it and pouring some anointing oil as a symbolic indication of the Holy Spirit.

6. The water should be sanitized for hygienic purposes because of the various brethren that will be baptized in it.

7. Pastors and ordained workers carrying out the baptism shall step into the water praying.

8. Each person shall be baptized by two pastors or ordained workers, one on each side of the person to be baptized.

9. The person to be baptized is lowered into the water with the officiating ministers saying the following: "I Baptize You in the name of God the Father, Son, and the Holy Ghost."

10. The officiating ministers shall submerge and immediately raise the person out of the water.

11. The brethren to be baptized, just like Jesus, should enter the water praying. Every person baptized must be issued a Baptismal Certificate duly recorded on the Membership database. Where there is no custom-built baptistery, a swimming pool or clean and safe stream can be used. Due to the cold weather in the United States, an indoor baptismal pool shall be utilized or an outdoor pool during summer months.

ORDINANCE OF MARRIAGE

Marriage is one of the mysteries of the Kingdom that is built on wisdom (Eph 5:23-30, Pro 24:3-5). The subject of marriage has become a most relevant issue in the world today, particularly as people all over the world have begun to take liberty for license—legalizing homosexuality and lesbianism, which, in the sight of God, is an abomination. Great danger lies ahead when one considers the biblical foresight, which points to men and women having sexual relationships with beasts. Man is unconsciously provoking the wrath of God, as it was in the days of Noah.

"If a man also lies with mankind, as he lies with a woman, both of them have committed an abomination: they shall surely be put to death; their blood shall be upon them. And if a man takes a wife and her mother, it is wickedness: they shall be burnt with fire, both he and they; that there be no wickedness among you. And if a man lies with a beast, he shall surely be put to death: and you shall slay the beast. And if a woman approaches any beast, and lies down there to, you shall kill the woman, and the beast: they shall surely be put to death; their blood shall be upon them" (Lev 20:13-16).

This is why the church must draw established boundaries about marriage in the light of scriptures.

Outlined below are biblical stands on marriage:

1. Marriage is God's idea, and it is ordained to be between a man and a woman (Gen 5:2, Matt 19:3-6)

2. Marriage is good and honorable (Heb 13:4)

3. Marriage demands a man leave his father and mother and cleave himself to his wife (Gen 2:24, Matt 19:3-6)

4. Marriage is between humans of the same flesh, i.e., human and human, not human and beasts (Gen 5:2, Mk 10:7, (Ecc 4:9-12), Eph 5:29-31, Lev 20:13-16)

Biblical Purpose of Marriage includes:

1. To provide a helpmate (Gen 2:18)

2. To reinforce the spiritual life of the spouses (Ecc 4:9-12, Pro 27:17, Matt 18:19)

3. To establish high-quality companionship (Gen 2:18)

4. To serve as a platform for childbearing and upbringing (Gen 1:28, 1 Tim 3:4-5)

5. To enhance human dignity (1 Cor 7:2)

Administration of Marriage - Member's Welfare

Scriptural facts must be fully understood before marriage can occur between two brethren. The Resident pastor shall monitor to ensure that the intending couple is well-monitored during their time of courtship.

Marriage is the consummation of a relationship in holy wedlock between two believers of the opposite sex (Gen. 2:18). For it to be properly consummated, the intending couple shall follow the laid-down process of this commission. First, they must make their intention known to the pastor, and afterward, they shall be committed into the care of the Marriage Committee.

Marriage Committee

There shall be established in every Local Assembly a Marriage Committee, which shall be appointed by the Resident Pastors. It shall be made up of between 5 members of proven integrity and with good marital testimony. For the purpose of continuity and stability, the committee shall be headed by an Associate Pastor but answerable to the Resident Pastor who oversees Marriage Affairs. Other members of this Committee shall be selected from the pool of ordained leaders or workers. Selected members shall include a healthcare worker and a legal practitioner where they are available. The Marriage Committee shall be responsible for the following:

1. To screen the intending couple in accordance with biblical standards for marriage.

2. To organize marriage seminars and counseling sessions and, where necessary, co-opt other mature couples as may be required.

3. To check the health status of the intending couples.

4. To receive written consent from the intending couples' families.

5. To receive any objection from within and outside the church in writing and follow it up accordingly.

6. To give and receive references in a situation where one of the parties involved is not a member of the church.

7. To present them to the Resident Pastor for approval before the final counseling/seminar.

8. To prepare monthly reports of activities to the Resident Pastor and to the LCC.

9. The tenure shall be two years, renewable only once.

Procedure for Marriage

1. Intending couples must be in courtship for at least three to six months prior to notifying the Marriage Committee.

2. Intending couples shall notify the church in writing through the marriage committee at least three months before the proposed date of Marriage.

3. Where members that intend to be wedded are from another local assembly, their Resident Pastor shall notify in writing the Pastor of the church where they intend to wed right from the inception of the Marriage process.

4. Intending couples shall complete marriage questionnaire forms accompanied by the following:

   (a) Two passport photographs each

   (b) Pre-marriage medical test results, which include Genotype test 3 months before the marriage

   (c) Brother's marriage proposal testimony

   (d) Sister's marriage proposal testimony

   (e) Brother's parental consent

   (f) Sister's parental consent

   (g) Brother's Believer's foundation class certificate (members only)

   (h) Sister's Believer's foundation class certificate (members only)

   (i) Reference letter from Senior Pastor/ Pastor In-Charge (for non-members)

   (j) Attendance of counseling session and marriage seminar

   (k) Marriage invitations should not be printed until clearance is obtained from the Marriage Committee.

   (l) Attendance of a marriage registry

(m)   Presentation to the church by public appearance one month before the actual Marriage date and display on all the church media platforms.

(n) Pregnancy test 2 weeks before the wedding,

Standard Marriage Preparation

Marriage is a holy institution; therefore, it is important that all activities geared towards it be done decently and orderly in line with biblical standards (I Cor. 14:40).

The following shall apply for all marriage preparations:

1. Intending couples are encouraged to have regular moments of prayer/fasting towards the success of the marriage ceremony and married life.

2. Intending couples shall not perform the traditional/engagement ceremony without the prior approval of the Marriage Committee.

3. As part of traditional rites to be fulfilled, all items that shall be presented must not be against biblical standards and Christian ethics, e.g., presentation of liquor.

4. Any activity or presentation during the engagement, marriage, and reception that can misrepresent the Christian faith, the Church, and the future of the intending couple shall not be allowed.

5. Dressing for all marriage events (i.e., engagement, marriage, and reception program) must be modest and decent to reflect Christian virtues (I Pet. 3:3-4).

6. The intending couple shall physically present the dresses to be used for the event to the Marriage Committee for sighting at least a week before the marriage.

7. The intending couple shall also participate in a marriage rehearsal, which shall be organized by the Marriage Committee one week before the Marriage Day.

8. The intending couple is advised to plan within their means and avoid anything that will lead to borrowing (Deut. 15:6, 28:12).

9. The intending couple must have modest accommodation in readiness for their married life.

10. The intending couple must abstain from any form of sexual activity until formally declared married in the church.

Following a review of the marriage application forms submitted to the marriage committee, each couple will be assigned to a specific counselor for a process of pre-marital counseling. This could be carried out by a Pastor or any ordained worker within the local assembly with an outstanding or proven marriage and family testimony. The need for this pre-marital counseling is rooted in the fact that the principles and the skills which make for successful family life have to be learned (Titus 2:1-8).

Purpose of Marriage Counseling:

1. To help prospective couples assess their readiness for marriage. Issues like backgrounds, socioeconomic level, maturity, character, and communication, among several others, will be addressed.

2. To teach the biblical guidelines for marriage. Every marriage should reflect the influence of Christ in the home: 1 Cor 13; Eph. 5:21-64; Col 3:16-21; 1 Cor. 7; and Pet. 3:1-7.

3. To stimulate effective communication skills. Counselees must be taught the value of spontaneous, honest, and sensitive communication. They should be taught to listen carefully as they try to understand each other and to talk through problems without it degenerating into quarrels.

4. To anticipate and discuss potential areas of stress, tension, and deadlocks. The challenges of adjustment when two people of different sexes and family backgrounds come together in a relationship like marriage are real and must be addressed.

5. To discover areas of deficiencies and assumptions and help provide lasting solutions. Watch out for knowledge deficiencies and never assume that the couple knows what they ought to. Provide adequate and relevant information, recommended books, tapes, etc., for their consumption or link them with others, e.g., professionals like medical doctors, lawyers, etc., who can provide accurate and more detailed and professional advice if there is a need for it.

6. To help provide answers for cost-effective, Christian, and healthy marriage plans. Encourage the intending couple to be prudent on expenses for the actual ceremony and to desist from borrowing and planning beyond the realities of their financial position.

7. To ensure that the marriage bed remains undefiled before marriage. The Bible states clearly that pre-marital sex is a sin and it must not be condoned. Talk about the negative consequences of premarital sex and offer practical advice on how to keep themselves chaste prior to marriage.

Counseling Format:

The following is not supposed to be a rigid, pre-arranged course. There is a need for flexibility, as some couples will require more time or attention than others.

I. Formal Counseling

A formal counseling session is to be carried out as follows:

1. Counselor acquaints themselves with the intending couple and their application forms.
2. Counselor follows the guidelines in the format provided. The approved checklists (see below) shall be verified and the compatibility of the intending couples ascertained; these include but are not limited to spiritual, medical, emotional, and socio-economic compatibilities.
3. Prospective couples need guidance and biblical instructions about marriage through the reading of books and listening to relevant messages; this will shield couples from experimenting with marriage entered. 2 Chr. 27:6. They must come to understand the need for adequate preparation.

II. Informal Counseling

An unscheduled visit to either of the intending couple by assigned member(s) of the committee is also recommended where necessary. It should be noted that a male counselor should be assigned to a male counselee and vice versa. The content of the counseling sessions shall include the following:

1. Effective preparation of couples for marriage and successful married life.
2. For encouragement and enlightenment.
3. To handle areas of confusion and deadlock.

4. To answer troubling questions.
5. To give direction and guidance on courtship ethics.
6. To provide productive advice on any area of observation.
7. To advise on handling parental issues and cultural differences.

Duration of Counseling

Counseling should start at least three months prior to the proposed marriage date. There should be six meetings of one-hour sessions prior to the marriage.

Documents to Analyze

During the counseling process, relevant documents to be reviewed include:

1. Parental consent forms
2. Medical test results
3. Marriage Registry Notification/Certificate
4. Approval report from your departmental leader

Recommendation/Report

At the end of the pre-marital counseling sessions with each couple, a letter of recommendation for the marriage should be written to the Resident Pastor. The letter should be a kind of report and should include details such as how many counseling sessions were done for the couple, the area of emphasis of the counseling, observations made about the couple, and how they were helped along those lines.

Marriage Seminar Topics:

The basic marriage seminar topics shall include, but are not limited to, the following as may be approved:

1. God's Concept of Marriage
2. Raising Godly Seeds
3. Communication in the Home
4. Family Management
5. Finance in the Home
6. Relationship with In-Laws
7. Sex in Marriage
8. The Power of Prayer
9. The Place of Fellowship and Church Attendance

Marriage Solemnization

Giving of the Bride:

[The minister instructs the father of the bride or his representative to stand beside his daughter]

To the father[s] of the bride[s]: Who gives this bride in marriage?

Response: I do

Minister to the Father of the Bride: Please take the bride, your daughter, by the right hand and hand her over to the groom. To the father: Please go back to your seat.

To the congregation: May I request the congregation to stand up as we go before the Lord in prayer: Our most gracious heavenly Father, we thank You for all the privileges of being in the body of Christ. We have come together to watch the miracle of Your love and the power of Your Spirit work in the lives of these people. We give You the praise, the honor, and the glory for the power of the

Holy Spirit in our lives to bring us into a place of union with the Holy Spirit and union with one another. We thank You for it, in Jesus' mighty name. Amen.

[The congregation may please take their seats]

Charge to the Bride[s] and Groom[s]:

As I read the Scripture from the book of Ephesians 5:22-32, I want you both [**all of you**] to pay very close attention to the words stated there. They are God's word that the Holy Spirit will honor as we stand on them in faith. The world has the idea that marriage is simply a legal contract [we do not make light of that]; but at the same time, it is a spiritual contract. When the word of God between two born-again believers is spoken, the power of God goes into operation. There is an actual miracle that takes place when the faith of these two [precious] people is released in God's power. God honors their faith and brings them into union together. With these thoughts in mind, listen very carefully to these words: Ephesians 5:22-32…

> *22 Wives, submit yourselves unto your own husbands, as unto the Lord.*
>
> *23 For the husband is the head of the wife, even as Christ is the head of the church: and he is the savior of the body.*
>
> *24 Therefore as the church is subject unto Christ, so let the wives be to their own husbands in everything.*
>
> *25 Husbands, love your wives, even as Christ also loved the church, and gave himself for it.*
>
> *26 That he might sanctify and cleanse it with the washing of water by the word.*

27 That he might present it to himself a glorious church, not having spot, or wrinkle, or any such thing; but that it should be holy and without blemish.

28 So ought men to love their wives as their own bodies. He that loves his wife loves himself.

29 For no man ever yet hated his own flesh; but nourish and cherish it, even as the Lord the church:

30 For we are members of his body, of his flesh, and of his bones.

31 For this cause shall a man leave his father and mother, and shall be joined unto his wife, and they two shall be one flesh. 32 This is a great mystery: but I speak concerning Christ and the church.

Charge to the Congregation:

In the eyes of Almighty God, these **[two]** precious people are washed by the blood of the Lamb – Jesus Christ of Nazareth. They have prayed and before the Lord God Himself, they believe with all their hearts that it is the perfect will of God for them to be joined in marriage. They have made their decision, so from now until the end of this age, I charge you to do everything in your power to see that this union remains solid, strong, happy, and prosperous.

Profession of Vows:

To Groom[s]: Do you take the bride as your wife, as your own flesh, to love her even as Christ loves the church, to protect her, and care for her the rest of your lives? [If you do, say Yes, I do]

Response: Yes, I do [Then turn to her, take her by the right hand, and make this profession of your faith]

To Groom[s]: I.. according to the word of God, leave my father and my mother, and I join myself to you, to love you and to be husband to you, from this moment forward, we shall be one.

To Bride[s]: Do you take the groom as your husband, submitting yourself to him as unto the Lord, showing reverence to him as the head of this union for the rest of your lives? [If you do, say Yes, I do]

Response: Yes, I do [Then turn to him and make this profession of your faith]

To Bride[s]: I .... according to the word of God, submit myself to you, to be wife to you. From this moment forward, we shall be one.

Exchange of Rings:

The minister requests the rings and offers the following prayer:

Heavenly Father, I sanctify these rings in your holy name and declare Your blessing upon them for an endless experience of love between this couple in Jesus' name. This ring stands as a symbol of marital identity. May this ring therefore link you to the covenant blessings of holy matrimony.

To be said by the Bride and Groom one after the other while the ring is placed at the tip of the fourth finger of the left hand: This is a token of my love and the sign of the vows we have made today in the name of God the Father, the Son, and the Holy Ghost. [**Now slide the ring fully into the finger**]

Pronouncement:

To Bride[s] & Groom[s]: [Join your right hands, please] As a representative of God, the Father, His Son Jesus, and the Holy Spirit of God, I now pronounce you ONE – together, as husband and wife. You can now remove your wife's veil.

Pastoral Blessing of the Union:

The Pastor steps forward and pronounces the covenant blessings of Deuteronomy Chapter 28:1-14 on the couple(s), and he lays his right hand on them without any further pronouncement.

Presentation to the Congregation:

Ladies and gentlemen, I present to you the newlywed couple(s), Mr. & Mrs. ……………………………………………

Altar Blessing:

In the event that the couple-to-be has violated the marital bed before their wedding or if it was determined that the couple has started living together before marriage, the Resident pastor shall call the couple in question, counsel, and encourage them to engage in Altar Blessing. The below-listed shall become the Creed of Prayer for the Altar Blessing.

Marital Consecration / Altar Blessing:

Marriage Creed:

A. **Charge:** - Gen 2:18-20 - For this cause shall a man leave his father and mother and shall cleave to his wife, and the twain shall be one flesh. Therefore, whatever God has joined together, let no man put asunder.

B. Today we are here before the host of Heaven and in agreement with both families that have agreed that their children should live and cleave as husband and wife. As a church community, therefore, having confirmed the aforementioned, hereby pronounce a blessing upon your lives.

Shall the couple kneel and the church stretch forth your hands and pray for them. The leading minister shall then pray for them, pronouncing a blessing upon them to continually live as husband and wife in peace and in harmony. Anointing with oil shall follow.

Afterwards, the ring shall be lifted and blessed.

A. For the Man: "My wife (name of the wife), I give you this ring today as a symbolic expression of my continuous love for you. With my life and body, I will love, care, and adore you as my wife, in the name of the Father, the Son, and the Holy Ghost." The ring shall be inserted in the fourth finger of the wife.

B. For the Woman: "My husband (name of husband), take this ring from me as a symbolic expression of my humble submission. With my heart and my body, I will submit, respect, and adore, in the name of the Father, the Son, and the Holy Ghost." The ring shall be inserted in the fourth finger of the husband.

To this end, we decree that your home is blessed, and your marriage is established in Jesus' name. Congratulations.

Wedding in Other Churches:

1. If, due to parental instructions or other acceptable reasons, both parties who are members are requested to wed in another church or denomination, they will still be required to pass through the counseling procedure of the church.

2. Where an intending couple is to be wedded in a non-Divine Touch Bible Church, if so desired, provision will be made for participation of our pastors in the marriage. For any couple who intends to wed in another local assembly, no reference letter will be given unless they have successfully passed through the Local Church Marriage Committee's basic screening.

Marriage to Unbelievers:

We encourage our members who may be seeking marriage, courting, or engaged to be married to an unbeliever (one who has not accepted Jesus Christ as Savior, rejects the Church and its teachings on sanctification, the Holy Ghost, and the tenets of the Divine Touch Bible Church) to reconsider and seek to marry one who is;

1. A member of our faith
2. Not antagonistic to our Pentecostal beliefs
3. One who will not hinder or handicap the Divine Touch partner, and children if involved, from adhering to our doctrine

Divorce in Christian Marriage:

1. Divine Touch Bible Church does not approve of divorce in Christian marriage under any circumstance whatsoever because it is not the perfect will of God for believers in Jesus Christ.
2. We therefore enjoin parties in a troubled marriage relationship to seek all scriptural means to secure amicable settlement in the home.
3. In view of scripturally approved available circumstances, a remarriage is encouraged in the following situations:

4. The saved spouse who has been deserted and divorced against his or her will by the unsaved spouse because of their belief in holiness and faith in Christ (1 Cor. 7:15).
5. The survivor of a marriage, that is, at the death of the husband or wife.
6. Widows and widowers are encouraged to trust in the Lord, pick up their lives again, and remarry.

Same Sex Marriage

We do not consent to same sex marriage as we believe that it is abomination and contrary to the word of God and outright disobedience to God; therefore, a sin against God (Gen.2:18; Pro. 18:22; Rom. 1:20). The church clearly condemns all forms of gay practice, lesbianism, homosexuals. We love everyone but condemns what the bible condemns.

HOMEGOING PROGRAM

Ecclesiastes 3:2 reiterates that there is a time to be born and a time to die. As believers, we were born one day but became born again. When a believer dies, we believe they have gone home ahead of other saints. We term it as a transition from this phase of life to another. As a result, we should be prepared as a church to lay the body of our departed brethren to rest. The following process applies.

Introduction

The Homegoing program is designed in honor of departed members of the Church (Psalm 116:15, II Chronicles 32:33). The following are the various stages and procedures:

Step 1 – Hospitality Team

On receiving the information about the departure of any member, the Hospitality team will make an immediate visit to the bereaved family on behalf of the Church. This team will be a standing committee whose assignment will be to liaise with the family until the final burial of the deceased.

Step 2 - Pastoral Visitation

On receiving the feedback from the visitation committee, which must be submitted within 24 hours, the Pastor or his Assistant will pay a visit to the bereaved family no later than three (3) days after the incident. In his visit, he is expected to effectively minister words of comfort and hope according to scriptural provisions such as in I Thessalonians 4:13-18.

Step 3 – Members Visitation

Information about the departed soul should be relayed to the Leadership of the church and also the workers' team. This is to allow close members to rally around the family throughout the period of the incident, visiting, praying, exhorting, singing, helping, giving, etc. Even where the departed is not known in any department, the team must rally around the bereaved family.

Note: There shall be no monies taken from the central purse of the church in the burial of the departed. However, members are free to financially support the family towards the burial of their loved ones.

Burial Programs

A full Commendation Service shall be held for the departed soul if the family so desires. This includes:

I.   Service of Song shall hold in the Church, Home, or any other place acceptable to the church (where requested, the casket may be brought to the Church for the service).

II.   Interment Service (At the graveside).

III.   Short Service at the family house after the burial.

Service of Song Program

Below is the sample program. Front page of the program with a picture of the departed soul.

Order of Service:

1. Opening Prayer
2. Praise & Worship/Songs
3. Hymn
4. Bible Reading: I Thessalonians 4:13-18

5. Biography (Brief life history of the deceased)
6. The Word
7. Special Prayer for the family
8. Announcement and Greetings
9. Hymn
10. Closing Prayer

(Please note that the maximum time is 90 minutes)

Interment Service (Service at the Graveside)

1. Opening Prayer

2. Hymn or Worship Song

3. Short exhortation at the graveside.

4. Interment: (The body is lowered with a chorus).

The Pastor makes the following declarations:

In faith and in the hope of resurrection to eternal life through Jesus Christ our Lord and Savior, we commit the body of our beloved Brother/Sister ………………… to Mother Earth. From the earth we came, and thence shall we return! Ashes to Ashes! Dust to Dust! "…And I heard a voice from heaven saying unto me, blessed are the dead who die in the Lord; yes, says the Spirit, that they may rest from their labors and their works do follow them."

5. Prayer and Benediction.

(Please note that the maximum time is 25 minutes)

Service at the Family House

1. Final Prayer for the Family – Short closing prayer for the family focused on comfort, peace, and protection.

2. Benediction.

Note: The bereaved are encouraged to resume church attendance immediately to hasten the healing process over the departure of their loved ones.

MEMBERSHIP WELFARE OPERATIONS

Every local assembly shall operate an annual welfare budget as may be approved from time to time.

Position Against Vows at All Levels

1. Levy in any form is an anti-covenant act.
2. It disconnects people from heavenly blessings.
3. The one and only financial obligation is tithing. Every other form of giving is as each one purposes in his heart.
4. Levying demoralizes those who do not have.
5. People should be allowed to give according to what they purpose in their hearts. We are not permitted to purpose for the people what they should give (2 Cor. 9:7-10).
6. Every giving must be done willingly (Ex. 35:4-6; 21-22).
7. When it is done willingly, the blessings flow freely and giving increases supernaturally (Ex. 36:6).
8. When it is not done willingly, the reward is lost (1 Cor. 9:17).

Sectional Ministries in the Church

Men Ministry

1. The men shall be married brethren or single fathers.
2. All names will be captured and stored in the database and online platform.
3. There shall be an annual men's/Father's Day event; this shall be in the church calendar.

Women Ministry

1. The women shall be married brethren or single mothers.
2. All names will be captured and stored in the database and online platform.
3. There shall be an annual women's/Mother's Day event; this shall be in the church calendar.

Youth Ministry

1. The Youth shall be unmarried brethren ages 21 and above.
2. All names will be captured and stored in the database and online platform.
3. There shall be an annual Youth Day event; this shall be in the church calendar.
4. Youth shall also have multiple spiritual growth meetings. This unit shall have a Coordinator.

Teenage Ministry

1. The Teenage ministry shall be children ages 9 and below 21.
2. All names will be captured and stored in the database and online platform.
3. There shall be an annual Teen's Day event; this shall be in the church calendar.
4. The Teen's ministry shall also have multiple spiritual growth meetings. This unit shall have a Coordinator.

Children Ministry

1. The children's ministry shall be for children ages 1 to 8.
2. All names will be captured and stored in the database and online platform.
3. There shall be an annual Children's Day event; this shall be in the church calendar.

4. The children's ministry shall also have multiple spiritual growth meetings. This unit shall have a Coordinator.
5. Children's services will be held concurrently with adult services.
6. The above Ministries hold an annual program. There is a set budget for each group, and that should be maintained.

Welfare of Members

The newborn

Upon the birth of a newborn, the hospitality team will pay a visit to the hospital of birth and also to the home of the baby's parents. A gift from the church will be presented to the parents upon the second visit. The amount to be spent should be at the discretion of the coordinator of the hospitality team. The Financial Secretary should be contacted, and a record/receipt should be kept. The visit will be completed by the hospitality team.

The sick and the afflicted

Visits will be made to the affected brethren, and an appropriate report will be brought to the Associate Pastor/Resident Pastor. The visit will be completed by the hospitality team.

The homeless and less privileged

In the event of such people in our midst, the resident pastor can secure hotel accommodations for two nights with a token of support for the two days. Such individuals should be referred to community support afterward.

The bereaved

Visits will be made to the affected families. Please note that no financial donation shall be accessed from the main church.

However, brethren can be encouraged to support the family of the bereaved.

FINANCIAL MANAGEMENT

1. The financial secretary shall collate weekly collections and deposit them into the appropriate account.

2. The total collation shall be reported on a monthly basis to the Resident Pastor. This account should also be made available to the Regional Pastor/Regional Coordinator.

3. The branch church shall continuously tithe its increase to the Headquarters church.

4. As a non-profit 501c3 organization, we are always open to IRS audits. As a result, all financial regulations must be handled carefully and records kept intact.

5. The church operates within a full and reasonable budget, and no branch church should spend more than 45% of its monthly income on running expenditures. Excesses should be avoided by all means.

6. There shall be a 2% reserve of the monthly income available for welfare purposes. In the event of exhaustion, it should be deferred to the following month.

7. Financial reports, including income and expenses, shall be made available to the general church on an annual basis.

MONITORING AND RECORD-KEEPING

1. Financial Records - should be kept and maintained by the financial secretary and given annually to the Resident Pastor.

2. Departmental Records - should be kept and maintained by all departmental leaders and submitted to the Resident Pastor at the end of the year.

3. Event Records - All events, including receipts, should be kept by the assigned leaders and presented upon demand and at the end of the event.

4. Program Records - All major event records will be kept per program and annually.

5. First-Timers Record - should be kept by the Head of the unit/overseer and made available to the resident Pastor.

DISAPPROVED PRACTICES

1. **DRESSING** - All leaders are expected to dress corporately for all services and avoid casual dressing. The same holds for all members of the church.

2. **VOW MAKING** - The church shall not compel any members or units to make vows and promises they cannot keep. All requests for financial donations will be on a voluntary basis.

3. **BORROWING** - should be avoided on behalf of the church.

4. **MERCHANDISE IN CHURCH** - Merchandising of all sorts should be discontinued and never allowed in the church auditorium and premises.

5. **FINANCIAL CONTRIBUTION** - The local way of contributing money to encourage savings is great but should never be initiated at the church at any level.

6. **CREDIT FACILITIES WITHIN THE CHURCH** - The church shall never be involved in any form of debt or usage of credit services. No one at any level should participate in that in the name of the church.

7. **USE OF UNGODLY LANGUAGE** - should be avoided.

BUILDINGS AND CAR DEDICATION

"Except the LORD build the house, they labor in vain that build it: except the LORD keep the city, the watchman waketh but in vain." - Psalms 127:1

"For every house is builded by some man; but he that built all things is God." - Hebrews 3:4

1. The church acknowledges that God is the owner of all buildings and provisions to purchase them, including car ownership.

2. Brethren are advised to present their homes and vehicles for blessing upon ownership.

3. The act of dedicating a building is a way of handing the structure over to God, the builder.

4. The main dedication of the building shall be carried out by the designated Ministers or leaders.

5. For a building, anointing oil should be placed in a bowl of water, and afterward, all parts and portions of the house will be anointed.

6. This also includes the interior and exterior of the house, including the main entrance.

7. For a car, the engine shall be anointed, and the presiding minister will place their hands on the vehicle and bless it.

CHILD COVENANT NAMING AND DEDICATION

Scripturally, a child is to be covenantly named on the eighth day after birth (John 1:59-63). Names are very important in the life of everyone. They are not only a means of identification but also a pathfinder to one's destiny. There is a spirit behind every name, and each time a name is pronounced, that spirit is released into action. Parents are therefore advised not to be sentimental but prayerful when selecting names for their children (Gen. 2:19, Gen. 49:1-28, Gen. 17:5, I Sam. 25:25, I Chr. 4:9-10, Luke 1:59-63).

Note should be taken of the following:

1. Names that are linked to ancestral deities and covenants should be avoided.

2. Avoid coining names that don't have meanings.

3. Avoid naming children after men of the world.

4. It is recommended that Biblical names with conviction of the Holy Spirit be given to your children.

5. Names in local dialects with covenant meanings are also recommended, but in brackets, the meaning should be spelled out as well.

Procedure

1. The parents of the child shall notify the Church of the birth through the Pastor or service unit leader.

2. A designated church official, who is an ordained Pastor, Evangelist, or Deacon, is assigned to conduct the naming ceremony.

3. A location and time should be chosen that will be suitable for the parent and the church official.

4. During the covenant naming ceremony at home, the parents of the new baby shall be required to be seated at a specific section along with relations. Movement in and out during the ceremony by the parents should be avoided.

5. The assigned minister delivers the charge of the day in line with the scriptures.

6. After the conclusion of the charge, the minister in charge receives the baby and the written names from the parents.

7. The minister in charge announces the names, which shall be repeated by the attendees, anoints the child with oil, after which covenant blessings are declared in the name of God the Father, Son, and Holy Spirit.

8. Offerings collected at the naming ceremony are presented as a love seed to the newborn baby.

9. The family is permitted to serve food and non-alcoholic drinks but not required in the event.

Child Covenant Naming Ceremony:

1. Opening Prayer
2. Praise and Worship
3. Welcome/Purpose of Gathering
4. Charge
5. Covenant Naming/Blessing of Baby
6. Offering/Presentation to Parents
7. Announcements/closing

The maximum time for the program is 45 minutes.

Covenant Naming Message

The assigned Minister is to exhort briefly on the importance of Naming and the Significance in the life of the child. Exhortation should include:

- The Significance of Naming
- Naming and Destiny
- Why we should give Godly names to our children.

Finally, conclude by letting all know that one's name remains forever; as a result, all attendees should ensure that their names are written in the book of life.

On the last note, give charge to the parent to raise up the child in the way of the Lord.

Child Dedication

1. Child dedication is done at the Third Sunday service in any Sunday of the Month.
2. Parents are encouraged to resume church attendance immediately after the child dedication, provided mother and child are physically and medically fit to do so.
3. In like manner, child dedication can be done any time after the child naming.
4. Parents of children to be dedicated must be members of the church.
5. It must be understood that we do not believe in baptizing infants or little children because the condition of salvation hinges on one's ability to believe in the saving grace of our Lord Jesus Christ.

DISCIPLINE

In the event of any misconduct, the following rules apply to different categories. You will be required to step aside for the specified weeks and stop whatever you are doing in the church. Gross misconducts are visible acts that violate the scriptures and the content of this Mantle. The goal of the discipline is to allow you to focus on your soul and find peace with your maker.

Ministers - 8 Weeks:

The Minister under discipline shall be under the monitor of the Regional Pastor. No Ministerial duty shall be awarded to any minister under discipline. Attendance to all services will be in place.

Leaders - 6 Weeks:

The Leader under discipline shall be under the monitor of the Resident Pastor. No leadership assignment will be committed into the hands of any leader under discipline. Attendance to all services will be in place.

Workers - 4 Weeks:

The Worker under discipline shall be under the monitor of an assigned leader or the Resident Pastor. All departmental functions will be suspended until the duration of the discipline is accomplished.

Members - 2 Weeks:

Any member under discipline shall be under the monitor of an assigned leader or the Regional Pastor. All operational units and functions of the affected member will be on hold until the duration of the discipline is accomplished.

LEADERSHIP SUCCESSION

1. The Church of Christ is a living entity. At any time that her overall leaders exceed age 70, the following applies:

   Direct coordination shall be handed over to the next trusted leader that is chosen by the outgoing leader/overseer.

   The outgoing overseer/leader shall serve in a supportive role as a mentor to the newly assigned leader for the next 6 months to a year.

2. Resident Pastors are under the 2-year rule, could be transferred or retained within their primary place of assignment.

   All transfers shall be total in this category; this shall include the resident pastor and his/her immediate family members.

   The church shall ensure the ease of transition to the new location.

3. Regional Pastors and regional overseers can also be transferred by the General Overseer from time to time.

DIVINE TOUCH BIBLE EXTENSIONS IN THE USA

The Church of Christ is expected to grow as a living church; in the event of a branch opening, it should be done in a wise manner to ensure growth and ease of transition. Branch opening shall occur in this manner:

1. The passionate need/Macedonia calls to a new location.
2. Site visit shall be conducted by the Regional Pastor and coordinator.
3. The Headquarters and the General Overseer must be contacted.
4. Prayers will be conducted to seek the face of the Lord over this potential new location.
5. Marching order or denial shall be waited upon. If denied, such location will not be considered; if approved, the Regional Pastor shall seek to get all the necessary registration in place.
6. Prayers, announcement, and mobilization commence towards the opening of the new church.
7. The Regional Pastor, with the approval of the General Overseer, shall determine who will be the leading Pastor of this new church.
8. A set day of opening shall be announced, and preparations continue until the church is born.

DIVINE TOUCH BIBLE CHURCH INTL INC USA - VISION AHEAD

And the LORD answered me, and said:

> *Write the vision, and make it plain upon tables, that he may run that readeth it. For the vision is yet for an appointed time, but at the end it shall speak, and not lie though it tarries, wait for it; because it will surely come, it will not tarry. (Hab 2:2-3).*

Every living thing must grow, and if there is no vision to guide the growth, the future will be threatened. By the Grace of God, the below listed in the MapQuest of our glorious future.

5-Year Plan

By the grace of God, within the next five years, we trust the Lord to:

1. Open at least 5 additional branches in 5 states.
2. Purchase 100 acres of land for our international base and annual program.
3. Purchase real estate for all branch churches in state-of-the-art buildings.

10-Year Plan

By the grace of God, within the next ten years, we trust the Lord to:

1. Train and ordain over 300 pastors.

2. Open more than 25 branches to make 30 branches in 30 states.

3. Purchase real estate for all branch churches.

4. Commence the Divine Touch Bible Church Intl base and city where annual programs will be held.

5. Establish a regional mega church building in the city and state the Lord shall choose.

25-Year Plan

By the grace of God, within the next twenty-five years, we trust the Lord to:

1. Have branches planted in the 50 states of America and in the diaspora.

2. Main campground will be situated on choice land and a city built for God.

3. Provide additional training for all ministers and leaders for the work ahead.

4. Organize annual programs where all sons and daughters will converge on a global scale in an annual event. The name of the event shall be tagged "Shammah".

Made in the USA
Middletown, DE
28 April 2023